# IRISH
# WIT & WISDOM

John Hickey
Martin Hintz
Cathy Ann Tell
Malcolm McDowell Woods

Publications International, Ltd.

John Hickey is business manager and cofounder of *The Irish American Post,* an Irish-American news journal with a readership of about 25,000. He spent his junior year of college in Dublin and is a graduate of the London International Film School. Hickey also has been publisher of his own small press that featured some of the Midwest's most prominent poets.

Martin Hintz is publisher and cofounder of *The Irish American Post.* He is a journalist and author with more than fifty books and hundreds of magazine and newspaper articles to his credit. For sixteen years Hintz was the promotions director of Milwaukee Irish Fest, which, as one of the world's largest Irish cultural events, annually attracts more than 100,000 visitors.

Cathy Ann Tell is a second generation Irish-American with more than 16 years experience as a writer, editor, and researcher. She has contributed to a variety of education, children's, and reference publications, including other compilations for titles such as *Pocket Inspirations* and *Teacher's Lesson Planner.*

Malcolm McDowell Woods, who was born in Scotland and raised in Northern Ireland and Canada, is a professional freelance journalist whose work has appeared in publications in the United States and Ireland. He currently edits a monthly food and wellness magazine and is editor and cofounder of *The Irish American Post.*

**Cover illustration:** Dan Krovatin
**Illustrations:** Dan Krovatin, Mark McIntosh

**Acknowledgments**
Publications International, Ltd., has made every effort to locate the owners of all copyrighted material to obtain permission to use the selections that appear in this book. Any errors or omissions are unintentional; corrections, if necessary, will be made in future editions.

Page 15: from *John Bull's Other Island,* 1907, Act IV, by permission of The Society of Authors, on behalf of the Bernard Shaw Estate.

Page 23: from *General John Regan* by George A. Birmingham by permission of A.P. Watt Ltd. on behalf of Althea C. Hannay and Susan Harper.

Page 66: Reprinted with the permission of Simon & Schuster from THE COLLECTED WORKS OF W.B. YEATS, Volume 1: THE POEMS, Revised and edited by Richard J. Finneran. Copyright 1933 by Macmillan Publishing Company; copyright renewed ©1961 by Bertha Georgie Yeats.

Page 87: Reprinted with the permission of Simon & Schuster from THE COLLECTED WORKS OF W.B. YEATS, Volume 1: THE POEMS, Revised and edited by Richard J. Finneran (New York: Macmillan, 1989).

Page 93: from *John Bull's Other Island,* 1907, Act IV, by permission of The Society of Authors, on behalf of the Bernard Shaw Estate.

Page 95: from *Children of the Rainbow,* © 1952, by Bryan MacMahon by permission of A.P. Watt Ltd. on behalf of Dr. Bryan MacMahon.

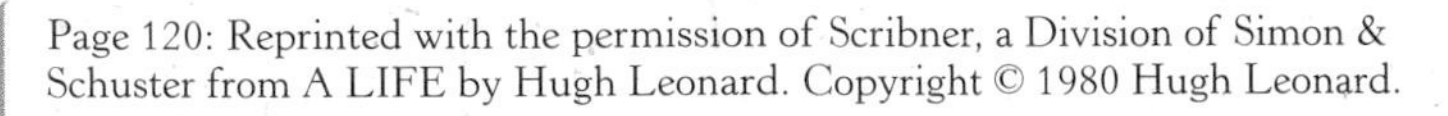

Page 120: Reprinted with the permission of Scribner, a Division of Simon & Schuster from A LIFE by Hugh Leonard. Copyright © 1980 Hugh Leonard.

Page 120: from *The Shadow of a Gunman*, 1958, by Sean O'Casey, by courtesy of the O'Casey Estate in care of Macnaughton Lord Representation Ltd., London.

Page 121: from *Man and Superman* by permission of The Society of Authors on behalf of the Bernard Shaw Estate.

Page 151: from *Pygmalion* by permission of The Society of Authors on behalf of the Bernard Shaw Estate.

Page 155: by permission of The Society of Authors on behalf of the Bernard Shaw Estate.

Page 163: Reprinted with the permission of Simon & Schuster from THE COLLECTED WORKS OF W.B. YEATS, Volume 1: THE POEMS, Revised and edited by Richard J. Finneran (New York: Macmillan, 1989).

Page 167: Reprinted with the permission of Simon & Schuster from THE COLLECTED WORKS OF W.B. YEATS, Volume 1: THE POEMS, Revised and edited by Richard J. Finneran (New York: Macmillan, 1989).

Page 174: from *The Humour is on Me* by Cyril Cusack by permission of Colin Smythe Ltd. on behalf of the Estate of Cyril Cusack.



Louis Weber, C.E.O.
Publications International, Ltd.
7373 North Cicero Avenue
Lincolnwood, Illinois 60646



Manufactured in China.

8 7 6 5 4 3 2 1

ISBN: 0-7853-2589-1

# Contents


## Introduction ☘ 6

## The Wondrous Isle ☘ 8

Welcome to the glorious land of Ireland, with its magnificent countryside and equally unforgettable weather!

## Ye Good Olde Daze ☘ 32

"Colorful" is probably the best word to describe the Emerald Isle's long, eventful history.

## Spooky and Not So Spooky Folklore ☘ 54

Leprechauns, fairies, banshees, the Blarney stone, and lots of legends you've never even dreamed of.

## People of the Auld Sod ☘ 88

Ah, those charming, bewildering, delightful Irish—what would the world be without them?

**Religion, Politics, and Other Irish Sports ♣ 122**

The Irish make sport of much that the rest of us find serious, but they're very serious about their sports.

**Glorious Words and Music ♣ 156**

In Ireland, homeland of poets and players, soaring notes and perfect verses are treasured above all else.

**Irish Chuckles and Groaners ♣ 174**

Wisecracks, witticism, and really bad puns from the Auld Sod.

# Introduction

PETER MARK ROGET must have been Irish. His thesaurus is as packed with synonyms for the Celtic personality as coins in a leprechaun's pot o' gold.

Let's start with a few, scattering words like the charms they are: Humorous, witty, droll, clever, sharp, and quick-witted come to mind. The Irish are also great at banter, twitting, japing, joshing, guying, and jollying, to say nothing of kidding, razzing, teasing, and jesting. There is almost a competition in word play when more than two Irish people meet.

According to ethnologists, sociologists, and other "-ists" in the know about Irish word play, the finely tuned traits of snappy comeback and nimble wit come from the verbal tradition of the Celts. This warrior race supposedly drove out the verbally poky mythological beings who lived in the lush, emerald green land of magic that was Ireland. Or maybe the Celts just out-talked their predecessors.

The Celtic bards, poets, and harpists all were revered during the centuries when the High Kings of Tara ruled this misty island. The isle's soft rains gave eager life to Irish speech, in addition to the land's thick grass. After all, what else is there to do when the cloud-heavy sky opens its soul with rain, but to stroll into a pub for a rest and a story?

*Irish Wit & Wisdom* pulls together just a hint of the innumerable tales and verbal ticklers spun by the Irish. Often, the chuckle is immediate. But listen closely for the wisdom embedded in the tale.

To come up with a wide-ranging perspective on all this Irish talk, the *Irish American Post* staff dipped into Irish history and surveyed contemporary Ireland, as well as rooted through its own files. The writers—publisher Martin Hintz, managing editor Malcolm McDowell Woods, and business manager John Hickey—drew from their personal experiences in Ireland and Northern Ireland, conversed with their contacts, avidly read the literary greats, and, of course, had a pint or two in the process.

In this book, you'll find fun stories about monks and saints, sage snippets of folk wisdom, gleeful snatches of songs, plenty of wry quotes, and loads of laughs. Politicians, authors, sports figures, and the ordinary Irish man and woman all have their say.

There remains one minor problem with a book like *Irish Wit & Wisdom:* There never seems to be enough space to add just one more great thought. The Irish imagination cannot be contained on the printed page.

But this will get you started.

—*Martin Hintz, publisher,*
Irish American Post

# The Wondrous Isle

IRELAND IS A small but insuppressible island half an hour nearer the sunset than Great Britain.

—*THOMAS KETTLE,*
*"ON CROSSING THE IRISH SEA"*

## Tales of Foynes

BRINGING ALIVE THE glamorous golden age of flight, the GPA Foynes Flying Boat Museum in Foynes holds a special place in the heart of anyone who loves travel. The museum is at the former layover site for the giant flying boats, which had their heyday from the late 1930s to the early 1940s. Foynes, a tranquil town on the River Shannon estuary, was a major international airbase before and during World War II. The community catered to traffic that flew between the United States and Europe.

On July 8, 1939, a Pan American Airways Yankee Clipper arrived at Foynes, making it the first commercial passenger flight on the direct route between Botwood, Newfoundland, and Ireland. International business travelers, famous politicians, spies, film stars, military personnel, and well-heeled refugees were regulars on the long flights.

The giant seaplanes had large staterooms, dining areas serving up gourmet food, and almost as many amenities as an ocean liner. However, the 41-ton planes were slow and seldom flew more than 500 feet above the ocean. Therefore, they had to lumber through storm and rain clouds because they could not rise above them. Because of strong headwinds, the planes often had to turn back. The flights could

not make emergency landings in the ocean because the 30-foot swells would break up any seaplane. Flights usually took 19 hours.

There are many Foynes stories but this is one of the most famous: Notified that a flight was due to arrive shortly after battling strong winds and stormy weather, the base chef decided to make up a welcoming drink. He wanted the guests about to land to be greeted with proper Irish hospitality.

He brewed some dark, strong coffee, added a healthy jigger of Irish whiskey, and topped off the concoction with a dollop of freshly whipped cream. The drink was ready when the travel-worn passengers eventually landed. Lip-smacking rave reviews immediately followed the first sips. Word of the fabulous new drink quickly spread around the world.

Thus was Irish coffee born.

## Soft Days

IT IS FOR good reason that you'll hear a lot of talk about the weather in Ireland. The Irish are used to cloudy skies and regular showers because they know that a puff of breeze will soon clear the sparkling air. A "soft day" is the euphemism for drenching rain, an all too frequent occurrence in the Emerald Isle for those not yet acclimatized to the wonders of the Irish climate.

A newly arrived visitor from the States was interested in learning the projected status of the weather. After all, he had rented a car and hired a guide for the week that he, his wife, and two friends were planning on touring.

"How has the weather been lately?" the Yank inquired.

"Not bad," returned the driver. "It only rained twice last week. Once for three days and once for four days."

THREE THINGS ONE should do every year—listen to a storyteller at a fireside, give a hand in a corn harvest field, and climb an Irish mountain.

—*MICHAEL JOHN MURPHY,* MOUNTAIN YEAR

# Cockle Soup

MANY RECOGNIZE the well-known refrain of the famous Irish folk song "Molly Malone": "She cried, 'Cockles and mussels alive, alive, Oh!'"

Cockles are small members of the clam family. Their succulent meat has been used for centuries by the Irish. This soup can be made with cockles or any other shellfish.

**4 dozen cockles**
**2 tsp. butter**
**2 tsp. flour**
**4 cups stock**
**2 cups milk**
**2 tsp. chopped parsley**
**½ cup chopped celery**
**salt and pepper to taste**
**⅓ cup cream**

Rinse the cockles well. Boil them in a large pot with salted water, preferably seawater. Once the shells open, immediately drench in cold water. Remove the meat from the shells. Melt butter in a saucepan, then blend in the flour, stock, and milk. Add the chopped parsley, celery, and seasoning. Cook for 10 minutes. Add the cockles, cook until hot, and serve with a small bit of cream on each serving.

## Getting Their Goat

EVERY YEAR, during the second weekend in August, the village of Killorglin hosts the famed three-day Puck Fair. The fair's traditions date back to long-lost centuries and is a summertime celebration of mischievous, mystical fantasy and fun. Killorglin is the first town encountered on the Ring of Kerry (a 179-kilometer circuit of the Iveragh Peninsula), one of Ireland's most popular tours for visitors.

The name of the festival comes from the custom of putting a billy goat (a puck) on a pedestal in the center of town and festooning it with ribbons. Pubs stay open until 3 A.M. under a special dispensation from the Garda, the Irish police.

FIRELIGHT WILL not let you read fine stories but it's warm and you won't see the dust on the floor.

—*IRISH PROVERB*

SWEET INNISFALLEN, fare thee well,
And oft may light around thee smile
As soft as on that ev'ning fell,
When first I saw thy fairy isle!

—*THOMAS MOORE, "SWEET INNISFALLEN"*

YOUR WITS CAN'T thicken in that soft moist air, on those white springy roads, in those misty rushes and brown bogs, on those hillsides of granite rocks and magenta heather. You've no such colors in the sky, no such lure in the distance, no such sadness in the evenings. Oh the dreaming! the dreaming! the torturing, heartscalding, never satisfying dreaming, dreaming, dreaming.

—*GEORGE BERNARD SHAW,*
JOHN BULL'S OTHER ISLAND

THERE IS A peculiar lightness in the air in Ireland, which brings healing on its wings to the over-excited mind, as well as to the exhausted body.

—*MARGUERITE POWER,*
*COUNTESS OF BLESSINGTON,*
THE REPEALERS

## Spuds for Everyone!

THE IRISH LOVE of potatoes is well documented. Boiled, mashed, or deep-fried as chips, the common potato is still a staple of any Irish meal. But one restaurant in the County Mayo town of Crossmolina goes even too far for Irish tastes. Each patron is treated not only to a choice of fried or boiled potatoes, but during the meal each and every table is served by a waitress whose sole job is to ensure that all guests eat at least two scoops of heavy mashed potatoes. One leaves the restaurant well fed, but dreading the next meal with its inevitable potato dish.

## Ireland

'TWAS THE dream of a God,
And the mould of His hand,
That you shook 'neath His stroke,
That you trembled and broke
To this beautiful land.
Here He loosed from His hold
A brown tumult of wings,
Till the wind on the sea
Bore the strange melody
Of an island that sings.
He made you all fair,

You in purple and gold,
You in silver and green,
Till no eye that has seen
Without love can behold.
I have left you behind
In the path of the past,
With the white breath of flowers,
With the best of God's hours,
I have left you at last.

—*DORA SIGERSON SHORTER*

TH' ANAM AN DHIA but there it is—
The dawn on the hills of Ireland!
God's angels lifting the night's black veil
From the fair, sweet face of my sireland!
O Ireland isn't it grand you look—
Like a bride in her rich adornin'?
And with all the pent-up love of my heart
I bid you the top of the mornin'!

—*JOHN LOCKE, "THE EXILE'S RETURN"*

BETTER TODAY than tomorrow morning.

—*IRISH PROVERB*

## Statuary Humor

THE RIVER LIFFEY flows down to Dublin from the Wicklow Hills and passes under 14 city bridges before pouring out into Dublin Harbor and Dublin Bay. Author James Joyce immortalized the waterway's spirit as the character Anna Livia in *Finnegan's Wake*. On O'Connell Street, a statue of a woman under a waterfall symbolizes the river's importance to the city. However, Dublin wits have irreverently tagged the sculpture, erected in 1988, as the "floozy in the jacuzzi."

## The Potato

Sublime potatoes! that, from Antrim's shore
To famous Kerry, form the poor man's store;
Agreeing well with every place and state—
The peasant's noggin, or the rich man's plate.
Much prized when smoking from the teeming pot,
Or in turf-embers roasted crisp and hot.
Welcome, although you be our only dish;
Welcome, companion to flesh, fowl, or fish;
But to the real gourmands, the learned few,
Most welcome, steaming in an Irish stew.

—*FROM* POPULAR SONGS OF IRELAND

## An Ancient Place

THE NAME OF County Wicklow is taken from the ancient Norse words *wyking alo,* which mean "Viking meadow." Wicklow is also nicknamed the "Garden of Ireland" because of its flower-festooned landscape irrigated by rivers and lakes. The town of Wicklow itself was founded by the Vikings in the ninth century, although a church was on the site as early as A.D. 430.

HOW SWEETLY LIES old Ireland
Emerald green beyond the foam,
Awakening sweet memories,
Calling the heart back home.

—*IRISH BLESSING*

MAY GOOD LUCK be with you
Wherever you go,
And your blessings outnumber
The shamrocks that grow.

—*IRISH BLESSING*

## A Cannonball Messenger

VISITORS TO Derry's St. Columba's Cathedral may wonder what a 300-year-old cannonball is doing in a church. But the bowling-ball sized iron sphere has quite a story to tell.

The cannonball dates to a pivotal moment in the city's past, when it took center stage in the course of European history—and paid a very heavy price for the attention.

In the seventeenth century, English settlers "colonized" Ireland. In Derry, the Protestant settlers erected a wall encircling the town overlooking the River Foyle. Those walls still stand and offer striking views of this bustling city.

In 1685, Catholic King James II ascended to the throne of England. He immediately began instituting reforms for Catholics everywhere in the kingdom, including Northern Ireland.

In 1688, Protestant William of Orange arrived in England with a contingent of Dutch warships, prepared to wrest the throne away from James. James fled to France, and William was crowned king.

James, eager to regain his crown, looked upon Ireland as his most promising battleground. In March, 1689, he arrived in Ireland with combined Irish and French troops. Gaining control of Derry would be a crucial first step in his bid to regain power.

It would not happen, however. Derry's settlers, alarmed by an anonymous warning letter, had previously closed the city's gates and would not allow James's army to enter.

On April 21, a siege began. Refugees swelled the city's population from 2,500 to 30,000. James's army of 10,000 men encircled the city, blocked traffic on the Foyle River, and waited. As days ran into weeks and then months, starvation and disease took their toll within the walls. The siege continued into the summer. On July 10, James's troops composed the terms of the city's surrender and fired them over the city's walls in a hollowed-out cannonball—the ball on display today in St. Columba's Cathedral.

On August 1, a fleet of ships was ordered by King William to carry relief to the people of Derry. After 105 days, the siege was over. Nearly 10,000 people had died within the city. James's troops lost 8,000 men.

☘

WHEN AN ARTIST goes to sketch in the West of Ireland, there is often trouble in getting a suitable place to stay. There are lodgings that advertise bed and board for five shillings, but you can't tell very often which is the bed and which is the board.

—*PERCY FRENCH,* MY FRIEND FINNEGAN

MAY YOU HAVE warm words on a cold evening,
a full moon on a dark night,
and a smooth road all the way to your door.

—*IRISH TOAST*

THE JEWEL most rare is the jewel most fair.

—*IRISH PROVERB*

AH, IRELAND . . . that damnable, delightful country, where everything that is right is the opposite of what it ought to be.

—*BENJAMIN DISRAELI, EARL OF BEACONSFIELD*

IN A LITTLE city like Dublin one meets every person whom one knows within a few days. Around each bend in the road there is a friend, an enemy, a bore striding towards you.

—*JAMES STEPHENS,*
THE CHARWOMAN'S DAUGHTER

WHERE THE tongue slips, it speaks the truth.

—*IRISH PROVERB*

THERE'S music there
And all kinds of sweetness
In the piper's greeting
At the end of day...

—*ANONYMOUS*

THE IRISH police barrack is invariably clean, occasionally picturesque, but it is never comfortable.

—*GEORGE A. BIRMINGHAM,*
GENERAL JOHN REGAN

## To Move a Sheep

THE IRISH HAVE always prized their livestock. In the days of the High Kings of Ireland, a man's worth was measured by the number of his cattle. Today, Ireland still allows cows, sheep, and goats to freely graze anywhere.

For one American tourist, this came as a surprise. Within an hour of his arrival in Ireland, his car was blocked by cows lazily moving down a busy road. As traffic backed up for miles, the herd made its slow, carefree trek to another field.

Then, going through Moll's Gap in the tourist drive called the Ring of Kerry, he encountered sheep. It was raining, and the flock apparently considered the narrow, unlit roads as a kind of manger. They were sleeping in the tunnels, huddled two or four deep. When he told this story at a pub that night, the Irish men laughed and told him to just keep driving. "If you hit one or two, it'll teach 'em a lesson. After all, we want to weed out the dumbest ones."

But the visitor hadn't the heart to "hit one or two," and he was worried about the damage to his rental car. Then one night, an opportunity arose for his revenge. He was walking along a path near the farm where he was staying. In front of him stood a lone sheep, escaped from the adjacent pen.

The American was scared. The sheep had that "why should I move for you" look in its eyes. Mustering up his courage, the visitor said, "Now, listen, I'm going to ask you just once. Please move."

The sheep did nothing and began to munch on a nearby bush.

"I have every right to use this path. Now, move," the visitor repeated. The sheep remained motionless.

The American sighed, pulled out his wallet, and withdrew a small white card. "I didn't want to have to do this," he said, "But unless you move now, I'm contacting my lawyer." With that, he threw the card at the sheep. The sheep reacted swiftly, scurrying under an opening under the fence and rejoining its bleating comrades.

The American picked up the card on which his lawyer's name was printed. "Works every time," he said to no one in particular. The remainder of his stay was very restful.

## A Giant's Story

FINN MACCOOL was great giant of a man and as such, he often had a great temper. Once it happened, so long ago that no one remembers when, that Finn and his neighbor got into a fine argument over who had the prettier view. Each sat on his respective mountaintop and disputed for more than a week.

Finn would argue "How can anything compare with this scenery? I can see the valleys stretching before me, wide and green, and the mountains rise up behind me each and every morning."

His neighbor would sneer back "Mountains and trees and grass. You call that a pretty scene? Look at mine, I don't just have the hills and valleys to look at, but I have rivers and lakes, and the ocean itself washes up against my land. Land never changes, but the water gives me something new to admire each and every day."

Now try as he might, and he tried for six days and nights, Finn could not think up an argument to counter his neighbor. It was true. Finn looked out every day and saw the same mountains and same trees and same grass growing dumbly. When Finn sneaked a peek at his neighbor's land, he saw the river calm once and then roaring after a storm, the lake deep and dark and then sparkling in the sun.

And the ocean, well, the majestic blue water almost broke Finn's heart.

Finn became furious, because perhaps his neighbor was right. So he flew into a rage and rushed onto the adjoining property. He took up a great handful of earth and flung it into the sea, where it landed and became the Isle of Man in the Irish Sea. And as to the hollow Finn had dug, well, that began to fill with water where the earth had sprung a leak. Soon Lough Neagh, the largest lake in Ireland, was formed. Finn was well pleased with himself, because now he had his own body of water to gaze upon.

WHAT WOULD A cat's son do but kill a mouse.

—*IRISH PROVERB*

## Causeway Mischief

BRITAIN'S NATIONAL TRUST looks after the Giant's Causeway, and sometimes makes a bit of extra money by charging a fee to companies that want to use it as a backdrop for film and photo sessions. The Causeway is a mammoth jumble of hexagonal columns of volcanic rock rearing from the ocean off the Northern Ireland coast.

Paul Waters, travel editor of the *Montreal Gazette*, reports that the editors of an agricultural magazine once got permission to shoot a picture of a prize-winning Ayrshire heifer posed seductively on the rocks. The Atlantic would be seething and foaming in the background.

When the day came, however, the heifer—a huge red-and-white animal—was less than enthusiastic. She had to be heaved and pushed out on to the rocks to have her picture taken. While the magazine crew strained and struggled against the noisily complaining beast, Philip Watson, the man in charge of the cause-way, was on top

of a nearby cliff. He was trying to explain the geology of the area to a group of Japanese businessmen. When he'd finished, he asked if anyone had any questions.

One puzzled-looking man raised his hand. "Why," he asked, "do men push the cow into the sea?" Watson looked down at the scene below him and then looked at his audience. He pondered for a few minutes how best to explain it, and then gave up.

"I told them," he said, "that it was an ancient Irish custom at that time of year to sacrifice a virgin cow to the sea to placate the Silkie spirits." The Silkies are supposedly sea fairies, often in the guise of seals.

And that's how some legends are born. Out of expediency, and because they often make more sense than the reality.

THE OLDER the fiddle the sweeter the tune.

—*IRISH PROVERB*

AN OLD BROOM knows the dirty corners best.

—*IRISH PROVERB*

## No Fish Here

HOPING TO LAND a few fish? Don't bother dipping your line into the River Boyle, in western Ireland. According to legend, St. Patrick once fell into the river and cursed it on the spot. The fishing has been poor ever since.

## I Want My Mummy!

AWARD-WINNING travel writer Betsa Marsh considers Dublin one of the world's top cities. A favorite stop is St. Michan's Church to view the mummies that are among the most popular, if not the most macabre, tourist attractions in Dublin. Bram Stoker, Dublin-born author of *Dracula,* supposedly received inspiration for his tale of horror by visiting the crypts under the ancient church.

St. Michan's was founded in the ninth century and has had a long, distinguished ecclesiastical career. It is also home to the organ keyboard on which George Frederich Handel practiced the "Messiah" before its Dublin debut.

But the mummies in the church's deep, dark underground vault are the main attraction. Four bodies are preserved there and can be viewed by the brave, the foolhardy, and the curious. One is a nun, another is a thief whose right hand and feet were chopped off, a third is that of an unknown man, and the fourth is a Crusader. Tour admissions and sales of souvenir postcards help with the church's upkeep.

There was a tradition that visitors could shake the long-dead soldier's hand for good luck, since it stuck up in a friendly fashion. The practice was ended when the poor fellow's index finger dropped off after one guest gave it a vigorous pumping.

Writer Marsh overheard one nervous visitor remark, staring at the dusty remains before skedaddling, "I was, ah, expecting something more Disneyland."

# Ye Goode Olde Daze

IT'S THE ONE place on earth
That Heaven has kissed
With melody, mirth
And meadow and mist.
—*IRISH BLESSING*

## Armed for Peace

IN 1492, an argument (the reason for which has long been forgotten) broke out between the Earl of Ormonde and the Earl of Kildare inside St. Patrick's Cathedral. Faced with superior numbers, the Earl of Ormonde and his men retreated to the Dublin cathedral's nearby chapter house, a small building where the church's clergy met to talk after morning mass. Once safely inside, Ormond had the thick oaken door slammed shut.

Luckily, a peaceful settlement was eventually worked out. But the inside earl still wasn't sure if he could trust the outside earl. So, as a tentative step toward reconciliation, a hole was chopped in the door so the two could shake hands. The first man to take the chance and extend his arm through the hole was the Earl of Kildare. After this bit of bravery, Ormonde relented and grabbed the other's hand for a vigorous pumping. The earls then became allies.

The incident led to the often-used English phrase "chancing one's arm," meaning "to take a chance on the unknown." By the way, the axe-hole can still be seen in the door.

IN IRELAND, we have a wonderful history, and, in many senses, an allegorical one. The allegory is of a small country which defined itself against the odds. Our ballads and our stories make much of this. And rightly. They commemorate the bravery and persistence which made us a nation. They give the account of the rooms and fields and back streets in which actions of enormous bravery were decided on and carried out. And as we read of them, we are left with the question of what it is that makes a nation.

*—Irish President Mary Robinson*

THE PRINCIPLE I state, and mean to stand upon, is this, that the entire ownership of Ireland, moral and material, up to the sun, and down to the centre, is vested of right in the people of Ireland.

*—James Fintan Lalor, Letter,*
Irish Felon, *June 24, 1848*

## A Sauna? No Sweat!

**A** PEAT-FIRED sauna? In Ireland? Well, yes.

Norse invaders came to the Emerald Isle in the eighth century. Not surprisingly, they brought a few of their favorite things along with them.

Which is why you may still stumble across a small, beehive-shaped rock building on a country walk. These sweat lodges were about six to eight feet tall with a small chimney hole in the top. A peat fire was lit for several hours to heat things up, then the fire was removed and rushes were spread on the floor to protect the feet of the one or two people who could crawl through the small entryway and fit into the tiny sauna.

Historians say the sweat lodges were used to treat various maladies, such as rheumatism and arthritis,

but surely they were also as good an antidote to the long, damp, and penetratingly bleak Irish winters as existed (at least until the development of enclosed shopping malls).

## A Revolutionary Introduction

POTATOES, WHICH WERE to become a staple of the Irish economy and diet, were first brought to Ireland by Sir Walter Raleigh from the New World.

THAT IT MAY please her excellent majesty to conceive of this her kingdom of Ireland, that it is one of the goodliest provinces of the world, being in itself either in quantity or quality little inferior to her realm of England.

*—CHARLES BLOUNT, 8TH LORD MOUNTJOY, ADDRESS TO ELIZABETH I, 1601*

BE MY EPITAPH writ on my country's mind.
"He served his country and loved his kind."

*—THOMAS DAVIS, "MY GRAVE"*

## An Adventurous Saint

THE LEGEND OF St. Brendan the Navigator is well known, and the story of his adventures could well be believable. Born in Kerry around 486, he studied mostly with Irish and Welsh saints. One of his avocations was traveling. It has been suggested that St. Brendan and his companions could have been the first Europeans to come to America, hundreds of years before Christopher Columbus.

Lending credibility to this tale, twentieth-century explorer Tim Severin followed the voyages of Brendan. He used the saint's original notebook and replicas of his boat and tools. After several excursions, Severin argued that St. Brendan may have landed on Newfoundland centuries before the Vikings.

COMICAL ERRORS IN speech were once known as "Irish bulls." A lady once asked the Provost of Dublin University, "Dr. Mahaffy, would you tell me what is the difference between an Irish bull and another bull?" "Madam," said Dr. Mahaffy, "an Irish bull is pregnant."

—*ORAL TRADITION*

## The Irish Staple

BY THE END of the seventeenth century, potatoes were the major crop in Ireland after their introduction into Europe from South America. Twenty-five metric tons per hectare were produced each season, enough for the vegetable to become a staple food in Ireland, Scotland, England, and Wales. The Irish economy became dependent on the potato. A typical Irish peasant family ate between 10 and 14 pounds of potatoes per person, per day, according to Triona Sherwin, curator of the Famine Museum in Strokestown.

These potatoes were of the "lumper" variety, normally used as animal fodder on the rich estates. But when combined with buttermilk, they provided adequate nourishment for humans. The more nutritious types were grown for sale overseas.

Fish often augmented the potato diet, but potatoes remained the basic meal, especially for the months when the seas were not navigable. And when the potato crops started to fail due to the ill-famed "potato blight," the fishermen sold their boats to buy food. So began a spiral that contributed to the Great Famine.

☘

## Historical Cheapskates

IN ITS EARLY years, Ireland was dotted with monasteries. During the Dark Ages, these remote abbeys served as places where learning and worship survived. But they were not immune from the ravages of warfare. Once the Vikings discovered that the abbeys possessed gold and silver, they became ripe targets for looting.

To protect themselves from the Viking threat, the abbots constructed hundreds of high round towers. The towers had one entrance, about 25 feet off the ground. When the monks were warned of an approaching war party, they gathered themselves and their treasures into the tower and scampered up the rope ladder. Then they pulled the ladder up after them.

Round towers are among the few buildings from that era still standing intact. But, at the famous monastery of Clonmacnoise in County Roscommon, one of the two round towers is only half complete. The story goes that one day, Owen, the mason, had almost completed his work and was at the top of the tower when the monks called up to him.

"Owen," the monks shouted up, "your prices are too dear. This poor abbey can't afford to pay you."

"Holy fathers," Owen shouted down, "my prices are what they are, and your abbey has more money than the county has cows."

"If you won't lower your fee, than you shan't come down either," said the abbot. Then the monks began to remove the scaffolding.

Owen was stuck up in the uncompleted tower for a day and a night. In the morning, he called for the abbot. "Father," said Owen calmly, "I have an idea. It is easier to pull down than to build a tower." With that Owen began to cast down stone upon stone. In that way, he could work his way safely to the ground.

With stones landing all around them, the monks grew alarmed. They prayed for Owen to desist and told him that his price would be paid. They rebuilt the scaffolding and Owen came down. But he refused to lay his hand on the work again. And, once the story got around about abbey's attitude toward paying its bills, the tower remained unfinished.

☘

## Shaky Beginnings for Greatness

THE IRISH HAVE not always been welcome in the United States, although they eventually proved themselves to be adept in politics and many other disciplines in the New World. The fact that they arrived in great numbers in Boston scared the locals. The Boston natives were concerned about the unsanitary living conditions of the new arrivals, forgetting that most of them were so poor they could not afford anything else. Boston was becoming a "moral cesspool," according to some incensed locals.

In 1850, Boston Mayor John Prescott Bigelow muttered that "foreign paupers [read 'Irish'] are rapidly accumulating on our hands." At rallies of angry taxpayers, the mayor lambasted what he called the "aged, blind, paralytic, and lunatic immigrants." One newspaper agreed that the "increase in foreign-born pauperism in our midst is an evil."

Of course, the Irish certainly rose above

those complaints by means of hard work, energy, enthusiasm, and drive to succeed. Within a generation, they had become the city's firefighters, police, judges, political leaders, business executives, leading clergy, and educators. They were able to organize, to lead, and—eventually—to take over.

"To a great extent, in their prolonged struggle for survival and achievement, they did turn Boston into 'an Irish city,'" writes Thomas H. O'Connor in his *The Boston Irish: A Political History*.

THE PROFLIGACY OF the age is such that we see little children not able to walk or talk running about the streets and cursing their Maker.

—*SIR BOYLE ROACHE DURING A DEBATE IN THE IRISH HOUSE OF COMMONS*

THE IRISH ARE a fair people;
they never speak well of one another.

—*SAMUEL JOHNSON, ENGLISH AUTHOR, 1709-1784*

## Queen Grace

THE COAST OF County Mayo is O'Malley country, and no O'Malley is more famous than Grace O'Malley, the wild warrior queen of the western province in the sixteenth century. Grace is now a mythic figure. An approving tale is told about how she acquired Carrickhowley Castle by pulling a fast one on one of her husbands.

MacWilliam Oughter, whose family had owned the tiny fortress for centuries, fell in love with Grace O'Malley. Grace accepted his proposal on the condition that either one could end the marriage within a year. In the following year, she brought all of the soldiers loyal to her into the castle.

At the end of the year, she refused to let poor MacWilliam come near her or enter his own castle. She then declared the marriage over by shouting "I dismiss you" at him from one of the castle's upper windows. She had no intention of giving back the fortress, and it was impossible to take it from her. The distraught MacWilliam left in despair, founded an abbey nearby, and lived there for the last four years of his life. As for Grace, she used Carrickhowley Castle as her base to successfully hold off English invaders.

In 1593, she sailed to England in her own ship to have a private meeting with another queen, Elizabeth I of England. Elizabeth wanted Grace to incorporate her fleet of galleys into the British navy, but Grace refused, although she agreed to stop raiding English shipping... for awhile.

Ms. O'Malley was also reputed never to blow her nose in the same handkerchief twice.

FOR SHE'S A great big stout strong lump
of an agricultural Irish girl,
She never paints nor powders
and her figure's all her own
For she can strike so hard
you would think you were hit by the kick of a mule
The full of the house of Irish love,
is Mary Ann Malone.

—THE AGRICULTURAL GIRL *OR* MARY ANN MALONE, *LATE NINETEENTH-CENTURY IRISH SONG*

## Legendary Settlers

ACCORDING TO SOME legends, Ireland was first settled by a band of exiled Greeks lost at sea. Their leader, Parthalon, had been exiled for killing his father.

## Feasts of Riches

THE COURT OF the Irish high kings were among the richest of the ancient world. Gold, silver, and precious gems adorned their clothing and weapons. Capes were trimmed with furs of badgers, foxes, and otters. Everyone at court was courteous, and prescribed manners were extremely important. In welcoming a guest, everyone in the room rose to their feet and often clapped their hands because the custom of handshaking was not known. The king greeted his visitors with a kiss on each cheek.

A guest would then be treated to a great feast, followed by entertainment from harpists, poets, jesters, and jugglers. These performers were always highly regarded and well paid for their services. One traveler wrote about the accomplished juggler of Conari Mor, saying he "had ear-clasps of gold in his ears; and a speckled white cloak upon him. He had nine swords in his hand and nine silvery shields and nine balls of gold. He throws every one of them up into the air and none of them falls to the ground, and there is but one of them at a time upon his palm; and like the buzzing of bees on a beautiful day, was the motion of each passing the other."

O SON OF God, it would be sweet,
a lovely journey,
to cross the wave, the fount in flood,
and visit Ireland:
to Eolarg Plain, by Foibne Hill,
across Loch Febail,
and listen there to the matching music
of the swans.
Flocks of gulls would fill with pleasure
as we sailed swiftly
into the welcome of Port na Ferg
in our 'Red-with-Dew'.
I am full of sorrow that I left Ireland
when I had my strength
and then grew tearful and full of sadness
in a foreign land.

—*POEM ATTRIBUTED TO COLUM CILLE, ELEVENTH CENTURY*

## A Bad Barrel

IRISH SOLDIERS fought on the British and American sides of the War of 1812, a bloody conflict that culminated in the historic Battle of New Orleans. There is a wry historical footnote about Irish-born General Edward Pakenham, killed while commanding the British forces on the day of the battle, January 8, 1815.

As was the custom of the era, his body was sealed in a keg of rum to preserve it on the long voyage back home to Ireland for burial. Somehow the keg was misplaced and the corpse was not found until several months later, when the barrel was tapped for use in a pub.

The Irish-born mayor of New Orleans at the time of the battle, Augustin Macarty, must have smiled as he imagined the panic at the bar when the rum-soaked general was discovered. According to some wits, this was a prime example of someone really getting "stiffed."

## Strongbow's Triumph

WHEN THE ENGLISH warrior Strongbow invaded Ireland in the long dim ages of the past, he had a difficult time taking the fortified town of Kinsale. So he resorted to a bit of subterfuge. He landed his main force on a spit of land jutting out into the sea known as the Hook. But he also brought a small force from another direction. This force had to march through a little-known village by the name of Crook. Kinsale fell soon after, and Strongbow said "I conquered by Hook and by Crook." And thus was born another notable cliché.

NOT IN VAIN is Ireland pouring itself all over the earth. Divine Providence has a mission for her children to fulfill; though a mission unrecognized by political economists. There is ever a moral balance preserved in the universe, like the vibrations of the pendulum. The Irish, with their glowing hearts and reverent credulity, are needed in this cold age of intellect and skepticism.

*—LYDIA M. CHILD, U.S. ABOLITIONIST, LETTER, 1842*

## Lord Chesterfield's Bird

THE NAME OF Phoenix Park in the heart Dublin owes nothing to the legend of the firebird rising from the ashes. In the 1700s, Lord Chesterfield, the British king's representative in Ireland, heard the local peasantry refer to the area as "Finnisk," from the Gaelic *"Fionn Uisge,"* which means "fair water." The park had many streams running through it at the time. The name apparently reminded Lord Chesterfield of the legend, so he set up a pillar on which a stone phoenix was mounted. From then on, the expansive park has been known by its current name.

WHEN ERIN FIRST rose
from the dark-swelling flood,
God blessed the green island, he saw it was good.
The Emerald of Europe, it sparkled and shone
In the ring of this world, the most precious stone.

—ERIN TO HER OWN TUNE

## Where There's a Will...

JONATHAN SWIFT, the dean of St. Patrick's Cathedral and author of *Gulliver's Travels,* died in 1745. He bequeathed money to build St. Patrick's a psychiatric hospital in Dublin. This was considered unusual for its time because the insane were usually ignored or locked in prisons where they languished.

But Swift had an answer penned before his death, one that he knew would answer any criticism over what he did with his money:

He gave the little wealth he had,
To build a house for fools and mad;
And shew'd by one satiric touch,
No nation [needed] it so much.

## A River and a Miracle

WHEN ST. PATRICK first came to Dublin, the daughter of the local king had just drowned in the river that divided the village in half. The king told St. Patrick that he would become a Christian if the holy man restored his daughter to life. St. Patrick prayed over the river and the princess lived. Her name was Leife and the river was thereafter called Leife's river or, as it is now known, the Liffey.

WE ARE ONE of the great stocks of Europe. We are the people of Burke; we are the people of Grattan; we are the people of Swift, the people of Emmet, the people of Parnell. We have created most of the modern literature of this country. We have created the best of its political intelligence.

—*WILLIAM BUTLER YEATS, SENATE DEBATE, JUNE 11, 1925*

I AM of Ireland,
And of the holy Land
Of Ireland.
Good Sir, pray I thee,
For of *saint charite*
Come dance with me
In Ireland.

—*ANONYMOUS, FOURTEENTH CENTURY*

IT IS SAID that western land is of Earth the best, that land called by name "Scotia" in the ancient books: an island rich in goods, jewels, cloth, and gold, benign to the body, mellow in soil and air.

The plains of lovely Ireland flow with honey and milk. There are clothes and fruit and arms and art in

plenty; no bears in ferocity there, nor any lions, for
the land of Ireland never bore their seed.
No poisons pain, no snakes slide in the grass, nor
does the chattering frog groan on the lake. And a
people dwell in that land who deserve their home, a
people renowned in war and peace and faith.

—*ST. DONATUS, FIRST BISHOP OF FIESOLI,*
THE LAND CALLED SCOTIA, *FIFTH CENTURY*

## Ireland Origin

EIRE WAS THE name of a beautiful queen who welcomed conquering warriors to the island. Many years later, when the Vikings were invading the land, their pronunciation of the soft sound came out as "Ira." So the people of Eire became Ira-ish and the island was known as Ira-land.

THE GAEL IS not like other men; the spade, and the
lom, and the sword are not for him. But a destiny
more glorious than that of Rome, more glorious than
that of Britain, awaits him: to become the savior of
idealism in modern intellectual and social life.

—*PATRICK PEARSE, IRISH NOVELIST*

# Spooky and Not So Spooky Folklore

THIS ISLAND IS a region of dreams and trifles.

—*GEORGE BERKELEY,*
THE QUERIST

## A Haunted House?

FOR MANY YEARS, there was a custom in Dublin to visit seven churches on Holy Thursday, offering prayers for both living and departed loved ones. After this vigil, the people would gather on St. Stephen's Green, standing opposite the house of Lord Iveagh and patiently watch one of the upstairs windows. If their vigil was rewarded, a cross would suddenly appear in the window. Then the crowd could go home with the knowledge that they had fulfilled a part of their Easter duty.

There are two explanations for the appearance of the cross. One version says that the Archbishop of Cashel was martyred on that spot in 1583, with the cross appearing as a remembrance of his death. However, the more popular story is told of a dying Catholic servant girl in Lord Iveagh's house.

Despite the girl's pleas, her Protestant master refused to send for a priest to console her on her deathbed. In desperation, the girl got out her rosary beads from their hiding place. But these, too, were taken from her and thrown out the window. The servant girl died soon after. From then on, the cross appeared in the window.

Of course, others have offered a more rational explanation. Once, when Lord Iveagh left the house, a Dublin carpenter went in to investigate the mysterious window. He found that it was not a window into a room at all, but instead faced the landing of a staircase. According to the carpenter, it was the outline of the staircase rails and banisters that made the cross appear in certain lighting conditions.

But surely no one believed such a wild tale as that.

THOUGH THERE IS no bone in the tongue, it has frequently broken a man's head.

—*IRISH PROVERB*

## Saintly Cuisine

ATCHEN was a lad who prepared meals for St. Patrick. Patrick later made him bishop of Bodony in Tyrone. Subsequently, Atchen has become the patron saint of Irish cookery, and many dishes have been named in his honor.

## Swan Song

SWANS ARE A protected and much revered species in Ireland. A famous Irish folktale, "The Children of Lir," touches on why the birds are so very special. According to the story, Aoife, the stepmother of the son and four daughters of the ancient King Lir, was insanely jealous of her husband's children. So she lured them to Lough Derravaragh (in today's Westmeath) to bathe. While they were splashing happily in the water, she cast a spell on them, turning the youngsters into swans.

The children/swans were forced to spend 900 years floating about on various Irish lakes. But the wicked stepmother eventually was sorry about what she had done, so she allowed them to regain their human voices and make wondrous music. It wasn't long before their father, King Lir, heard about the

talking swans and decreed that, forever after, no swans should be killed in Ireland.

Christianity arrived in Ireland about the time the children's magical sentence was up as swans. After they were reincarnated as humans (but much older and timeworn), they were baptized.

And what happened to the nasty Aoife? Supposedly, her own father, King Dearg, learned what she had done and turned her into a demon.

WHEN DEATH comes, it will not go away empty.

—*IRISH PROVERB*

THERE IS NO fireside like your own fireside.

—*IRISH PROVERB*

MAY THE FACE of every good news
And the back of every bad news
Be towards us.

—*IRISH BLESSING*

## A Big Fish Story

MULROY BAY IN County Donegal has often been compared to the fjords of Norway. The region's beauty is a big draw, and travelers come from all over Ireland for the scenery along the inlet. But hardly anyone brings along a fishing pole.

Locals say there have been very few fish in the bay's waters since the days of St. Colmcille. Seems the great saint one day approached a group of fishermen on the shore of the bay, blessed them, and asked how the day's fishing had gone.

Poorly, they replied, even though they had actually made quite a haul of trout and salmon that day.

Saint Colmcille, however, was onto the fib. "If you caught no fish today, may you catch them now," he said. "If you did catch fish today, may you never catch them again." And to this day, say the locals, trout and salmon have all but disappeared from Mulroy Bay.

Then again, perhaps it's all a big fish story, a way to keep other anglers away.

A GOOD WORD never broke a tooth.

—*IRISH PROVERB*

## A Deep Subject

WELLS ARE especially prized in Ireland, be they blessed by some saint as holy or merely for the clear water they supply. Tradition has it that the well can also be a prophet where matters of the heart are concerned.

If a young woman wishes to know whether her affections will be returned, she consults the neighborhood well. As night falls, the maid should drop a small tin cup called a noggin into the well and speak the name of her beloved. She should depart immediately, leaving the well to work its magic for the night. If she wants the answer, she must return to the spot exactly at daybreak. If the noggin is found floating on the surface, she is assured of her heart's desire. But if the cup is not to be found, then her hopes have probably sunk with it to the bottom of the well.

## Hungry Grass

MANY COUNTRY PEOPLE always take a small piece of bread with them when walking for fear of stumbling onto a patch of the "hungry grass." This legend sprang from the tragic experience of the Great Famine in the 1840s.

The story goes like this: A healthy man or woman strolling in the Irish countryside takes a shortcut through an unknown field. Suddenly, the stomach begins to ache. This is swiftly followed by an indescribable weakness that buckles the knees and causes a loss of sight. The only cure is small bit of bread. Upon eating, the symptoms disappear.

The "hungry grass" is described as white and herblike in appearance. It is said that these patches are the places where the victims of the famine could go no further and lay down to die.

## Fairy Places

IRISH FIELDS have been plowed and planted for thousands of years. The rocks have been removed, usually by hand, and now form the hundreds of stone fences that wall off even the smallest property. Yet in many of those fields, one may see a small mound of brush, hawthorn, and stone rising defiantly amid the carefully tended furrows.

These ancient stone circles are the "fairy rings" still respected by farmers as part of a different world. For while cows and sheep may gnaw on the gorse and hawthorn, no plow or tractor will disturb these magical spots. It wouldn't pay to bother the spirits at their rest. And at night, who knows what mischief an angry fairy can cause.

HE HAMMERED AND sang with tiny voice,
And sipped his mountain dew;
Oh! I laughed to think he was caught at last,
But the fairy was laughing, too.

—*ROBERT DWYER JOYCE, "THE LEPRECHAUN"*

## Fairy Tricks

OCCASIONALLY, THE fairies fancy human babies and carry them away to their own magic kingdom. They leave behind a "changeling," a sickly fairy child or a log of oak that looks like a person pining away.

## Beware the Banshee!

THE BANSHEE ARE a peculiarly Irish sort of ghost. Originally, they were beautiful young maidens who carried away potential suitors to Tir-na-nog, the land of perpetual youth. Eventually, the pretty girls evolved into the screeching, withered hags with wild eyes and flaming hair known as the banshee.

The banshee appear to those whose death is imminent. They beckon the doomed into that unknown spirit world with shrieks of terror, described as a drowned-out wailing of a tormented soul. It is said that the banshee haunt only those who can trace their roots to the ancient royal Irish families. One can only wish to be spared this inheritance.

## An Ill Omen

IF YOU SPOT a tiny ball of light following you, watch out. Celtic legend tells of "corpse candles," tiny pillars of flame that travel low over the ground and journey from a graveyard to the home of an unfortunate person, then back to the cemetery.

The visit is most definitely not an honor. The corpse candle is considered an omen of death, and the poor soul paid the visit, well, he may want to check up on his insurance policy.

## Beware of Dog!

IF YOU ENCOUNTER a black dog with blazing red eyes, quickly make the sign of the cross. The dog will leap in the air and disappear, for it is merely the devil in disguise.

## Knock Three Times...

IT IS A tradition in the west of Ireland that three knocks on the cottage door warn that a member of the family will soon die.

GOOD ENOUGH for who it's for.

—*COUNTY CLARE PROVERB*

## Thorny Advice

DON'T DISTURB THE single thorn tree growing in a field. Legend has it the shrub is almost certainly inhabited by fairies, and they will make your life miserable should you cut it down.

Even today, hawthorns are almost never intentionally felled. A hawthorn known as St. Ciaran's Bush stands smack in the middle of a road leading from Birr to Kinnitty.

I CARRY THE sun in a golden cup,
The moon in a silver bag.

—*WILLIAM BUTLER YEATS,*
*"THOSE DANCING DAYS ARE GONE"*

## A Remarkable Herb

LEEKS HAVE LONG been a hardy staple of the Irish diet. In fact, they were once considered so essential to the peasants that it was natural to attribute the plant's introduction to Ireland to St. Patrick himself.

St. Patrick was at the bedside of a dying woman when the woman raised herself up and pointed to the space in front of her.

"What is it you see?" asked St. Patrick. "I see an herb," gasped the woman, "and unless I eat it I will die." St. Patrick saw nothing, but asked, "What does the plant resemble?" The woman said, "It is like rushes."

St. Patrick then blessed a group of rushes outside the cottage and they became leeks. The woman ate the leeks and lived.

## Full House

LEAP CASTLE IN County Offaly is reported to house more haunts than any other castle in Ireland, with 24 ghosts rattling through its ancient halls.

## Grave Matters

ACCORDING TO IRISH superstition, if a tombstone is not placed on a grave within a year, the next of kin will die.

## Fairy Music

IRISH DANCE AND music are celebrated throughout the world. It is said that their inspiration does not come from mortals, but from the fairies. A story is told in County Clare about this fairy music.

A young man named Colin returned to his cottage after a long day of cutting peat. He found a young woman named Kathleen sitting by his fire. She was softly humming a sad tune. Colin had never seen the beautiful woman before, but he immediately fell in love with her.

He asked, "What is that lovely, sad song you're singing?"

The young woman looked at him blankly, as if she had only just noticed that he was there. "I've lost it," she said.

"Lost what?" Colin asked.

"I've been with fairies," she said. "I was going to the well when I slipped and fell. When I got up, it was like the hills glowed. Then I heard it, the fairy music. It was soft and pretty and low and beautiful. Then I forgot why I'd come to the well and forgot my da and ma and the little ones waiting for me.

"The music charmed me, you see. Then there were fairies all around me. Beautiful people they were, dressed in silver and gold. They were dancing to the sweetest music. Then a young man took my hand and we danced 'til the moon and the stars left the sky. It was like floating on the air. The young man was a fairy prince.

"But then a man with flaming red hair thrust a branch of ivy into my hands. He said only one thing, 'Remember.' All my life came rushing back to me and I got scared. I started to run. I could hear the fairies coming so I ran harder."

Colin said, "But you got away. There are no fairies here to scare you anymore. You won't be lost for long."

The young woman looked up at Colin with tears in her eyes. "No, you don't understand. It's the fairy music I've lost. There's a memory of it in my head, but I can't find it. If I don't hear it again, I'll die."

So Colin took her into his life and she became his wife. They were very happy. But every full moon, Kathleen stepped outside and sang her unknown song to herself, trying to find the words and melody to the lost fairy music.

☘

## To Tell the Truth...

AMID THE RUINS of a monastery on one of the many islands dotting Ireland's western shores lies an ancient black marble flagstone. The monks who lived there hundreds of years ago gave the stone the power of the *Cremave,* or the Swearing Stone. From around the country, anyone suspected of a sin or crime was brought before the stone to testify to his or her actions. Even today, there are those who believe that if the accused swears falsely, the stone has the power to set a mark upon the person's face. If no mark appears, the person is innocent.

One time, a murder had been committed near the island. The neighbors suspected one man, but did not have proof. This did not stop them from going to the man's cottage, binding him, and taking him before the Swearing Stone. The people said, "If he is innocent, the *Cremave* will clear him. If he is guilty, let him suffer for his crimes." The man appeared before the stone with his accusers. There they were met by a priest who said, "Speak the truth before your friends and before the face of God."

The man laid his hand upon the stone and swore that he was innocent. Instantly, his right arm shriveled and he fainted dead away. The stone had enacted its punishment; the man lived as a miserable cripple to the end of his days. The people took no more actions against him for they knew the stone would visit more suffering on the man and his family.

A few weeks later, a daughter was born to the man and his wife. On her brow, she bore the imprint of a bloody hand. This stayed with her for the rest of her life. And every one of the murderer's descendants had a similar mark until the seventh generation, which was born clean of man's guilt and perjury.

## Blarney Castle

THERE IS A boat on the lake to float on,
And lots of beauties which I can't entwine;
But were I a preacher, or a classic teacher,
In every feature I'd make 'em shine!
There is a stone there, that whoever kisses,
O! he never misses to grow eloquent;
'Tis he may clamber to a lady's chamber,
Or become a member of parliament:
A clever spouter he'll soon turn out, or
An out-and-outer, "to be let alone."
Don't hope to hinder him, or to bewilder him,
Sure he's a pilgrim from the Blarney stone!

—*Father Prout (Frances Sylvester Mahony)*

## The Faeries

UP THE AIRY mountain,
Down the rushy glen
We daren't go a-hunting
For fear of little men;
Wee folk, good folk,
Trooping all together;
Green jacket, red cap,
And white owl's feather
Down along the rocky shore
Some make their home
They live on crispy pancakes
Of yellow tide-foam
Some in the reeds
Of the black mountain lake,
With frogs for their watch-dogs
All night awake.
High on the hill-top
The old King sits;
He's now so old and gray
He's nigh on lost his wits
With a bridge of white mist
Columbkill he crosses,
On his stately journeys
From Slievleague to Rosses;
Or going up with music

On cold starry nights,
To sup with the Queen
Of the gay Northern lights.
By the craggy hill-side,
Through the mosses bare,
They have planted thorn-trees,
For pleasure here and there
Is any man so daring
As dig them up in spite,
He shall find their sharpest thorns
In his bed at night.
Up the airy mountain,
Down the rushy glen,
We daren't go a-hunting
For fear of little men,
Wee folk, good folk,
Trooping all together;
Green jacket, red cap,
And white owl's feather.

—*BY WILLIAM ALLINGHAM AS TOLD TO WILLIAM BUTLER YEATS FOR HIS COLLECTION ENTITLED* IRISH FOLK STORIES AND FAIRY TALES

☘

## Love Among the Herbs

THE IRISH ARE said to be the last of the great ancient Celtic nations to still possess the strange secrets of those herbs that can cure disease, cause love or hatred, or reveal the hidden mysteries of life and death.

Perhaps the most powerful and dangerous herbal remedy was the love potion, for its effects were often unpredictable. One handsome youth of the finest character and conduct suddenly became wild and reckless after the love potion was administered by a young girl who was passionately in love with him. They were married, but the young man led a disorderly life of drunken brawls and odd jobs. The girl turned into a nervous old woman who acted as if she lived under a constant terror. She never smiled again.

If you dare, here is one simple potion guaranteed to cause love. Keep a sprig of mint in your hand till the herb grows moist and warm, then take hold of the hand of the person you love, and he or she will follow you forevermore. No magic words are needed, but silence must be kept between the two parties for ten minutes to give the charm time to work.

## A Bridge of Great Fortune

THERE IS A bridge in Athlone that has many legends about it. Here is one story about the celebrated old bridge.

A gentleman, living in the western part of Ireland, dreamed one night that if he went to Athlone and walked upon its bridge for a few hours, he would make his fortune. He dreamed the same dream three times in succession, which assured him that certainly good luck was to follow. He told his wife about the dreams, and she urged him to go.

As he was walking the bridge, a local man asked him why he was pacing back and forth across the span. The gentleman told him of the dreams.

"Oh, that's nothing," said the stranger. "I dreamt three times that if I went to a certain man's garden in the west (naming the gentleman's own property), I'd find a crock of gold under the oldest apple tree in the orchard."

The westerner rushed home immediately and dug for the crock. He found the pot, brimming over with ancient gold coins. This established his fortune, and his descendants, it is claimed, still enjoy the fruits of that inheritance.

## The King of Cats

THE IRISH HAVE a legend that ensures that their cats will be well treated. For the common household cat may be the King of the Cats, a cat with magical powers. Since there is no distinguishing mark of his rank, it is difficult to verify any cat's royal standing. The best way is to cut off a tiny bit of ear. If your cat is really the King of the Cats, he will immediately speak out and tell you some very disagreeable truths about yourself.

One Irishman, furious because the milk for his morning tea was missing again, cut off the head of the family cat and threw it on the fire. While the flames licked at its fur, the head exclaimed, "Go tell your wife that you have cut off the head of the King of the Cats. But I shall come back and be avenged for this insult."

One year later, as the master was playing with the family's new pet kitten, it suddenly flew at his throat and bit him so severely that he died the next day.

## The Fairy Shoemaker

LEPRECHAUNS ARE easily recognizable by their clothing and habits. Unlike the trouping fairies who wear green jackets, the solitary leprechaun wears a red coat with seven rows of buttons with seven buttons in each row. In Ulster, in the far north of Ireland, the leprechauns also wear cocked hats. The southern leprechauns regularly have a white owl's feather in their red cloth caps.

The leprechauns are mainly mischievous but can be quite nasty if surprised by a human trying to capture them. They are prone to leaping in the air, balancing on the point of their hats with their heels in the air, and generally cavorting around. This fairy is among the tallest of the Irish sprites, standing between two and three feet high.

The leprechaun is the fairy shoemaker and is usually seen with the tools of its trade: an awl, shoe nails, and a hammer tucked into its belt. Sometimes, it wears a leather apron. Because of its skilled trade, the leprechaun is the wealthiest of the fairies, hiding its pots of gold all over Ireland.

## Creatures of Legend

THE MERROWS are Irish sea creatures. Their name comes from the words *muir* (sea) and *oigh* (maid). They are found only along the wilder, remote coasts of Ireland. Fishermen do not want to see merrows when they set out in their curraghs, or fishing boats, because it always means a storm is coming.

Merrows are not difficult to identify. The males have green teeth, emerald-colored hair, pig's eyes, and red noses. But the female merrows are beautiful, even though they have a fish-like tail and duck-like webbing between their fingers.

It is easy to fall in love with a female merrow. And often the females watch for the most handsome fishermen to lure them away from their wives and lovers on land. Sometimes, the merrows come out on land

and wander around the countryside shaped like a yearling cow. They then slip back out to sea when confronted by a human.

'TIS I GO Fiddling, Fiddling

'Tis I go Fiddling, Fiddling,
By weedy ways forlorn:
I make the blackbird's music
Ere in his breast 'tis born:
The sleeping larks I waken
Twixt the midnight and the morn.
No man alive has seen me,
But women hear me play
Sometimes at a door or window,
Fiddling the souls away,—
The child's soul and the colleen's
Out of the covering clay.
None of my fairy kinsmen
Make music with me now:
Alone the rates I wander
Or ride the whitethorn bough
But the wild swans they know me,
And the horse that draws the plough.

—*NORA HOPPER*

## More Banshee Lore

THE BANSHEE IS an attendant fairy that follows old families in Ireland and wails before a death. The word comes from *ban* (pronounced "bean"), which means "a woman," and *sidhe* (pronounced "shee"), which means "fairy." The *caoine* (keen) is the funeral cry in Ireland; it is said to be an imitation of the banshee's howling. When more than one banshee is present, they sing in chorus, which is the prelude to the death of a great person. Sometimes, the banshee rides in a large black coach, mounted by a coffin and pulled by a headless horse. If you open your door when the coach rumbles past your house, a bucket of blood might be thrown in your face.

## Some Useful Charms

ONE CAN NEVER be too careful, with all the trouble, turmoil, lost love, and sickness in the world. A good Irish charm might be just the thing to improve your day. Here are a few that have proven effective over the centuries... or so we've been told.

Sickness: Turn the bed north to south, with the head to the north.

Money: Carry the back tooth of a horse in your pocket, and soon the money will come.

Luck in Cards: Stick a crooked pin in the lapel of your coat.

Beauty: Wash your face in May Day dew just when the sun rises.

Dreams: For a dream to come true, always tell it first to a woman named Mary.

Ghosts: A ghost cannot cross a running stream.

Toothache: (prevention) Never comb your hair on a Friday and never shave on a Sunday. (cure) Take a handful of grass from a grave you have prayed over and chew it well, being careful not to swallow.

Love: Offer a drink to your beloved and, as he or she drinks, say to yourself three times: "Your face to my face and your head turned from all others. You for me, and me for thee, and for none else."

THERE ARE FINER fish in the sea
than have ever been caught.

—*IRISH PROVERB*

## A Ring Around Your Heart

YOU CAN FIND the popular claddagh ring at most jewelry stores these days, but few folks know the real story behind this piece of jewelry.

The ring's design features two hands holding a crowned heart, and it originated in the old fishing village of Claddagh near Galway. The inhabitants remained completely apart from the rest of Ireland by their custom of marrying only those from the village.

For many families who lived in the region, the rings were heirlooms, passed from mother to daughter. Worn on the right hand with the heart pointing toward the fingertips, it meant the woman was available. Wearing the ring on the left hand with heart pointing toward the wrist meant she was engaged.

## Mother Told You Not to Stare!

IF YOU ARE caught gazing at any person or thing while in Ireland, be sure to say "God bless!" for you may accused of giving the dreaded Evil Eye to the object of your gaze. Or if someone gives you the Evil Eye, use this prayer that St. Bridget wrote and hid in her hair for such an occasion: "If fairy, man or woman hath overlooked ye, remember there are three greater in heaven who will cast all evil into the great and terrible sea. Amen."

THERE'S A DEAR little plant that grows in our isle,
'Twas St. Patrick himself sure that set it.
It thrives through the bog, through the brake,
and the mireland;
And he called it the dear little shamrock of Ireland.

—*ANDREW CHERRY,*
*"THE GREEN LITTLE SHAMROCK"*

MAY YOU HAVE the hindsight
to know where you've been
and foresight to know where you're going
and the insight to know when you're going too far.

—*IRISH TOAST*

THE EYE OF a friend is a good looking glass.

—*IRISH PROVERB*

## A Bunch of Blarney

FOR GENERATIONS, kissing the Blarney Stone has been considered the ultimate in achieving the ability to chatter at great length . . . and all done with a twinkle in the eye. There are many versions as to how this chunk of limestone in southern Ireland earned its reputation as the world's best-known site for "kiss 'n' tell." According to one, it was England's Queen Elizabeth I who coined the well-known "blarney" phrase, simply out of sheer exasperation.

Lord Blarney, who was master of the castle that bore his name near Cork, apparently had the energetic—and limitless—ability to talk endlessly in circles, without ever really answering the queen's questions. "That's Blarney," her royal highness allegedly was heard to mutter regularly whenever the Irish peer prattled on.

The stone itself is part of the upper rampart in Lord Blarney's ancient homestead, which dates back to 1446. The place is in ruins now, the victim of time and an admirable Irish penchant for leaving a good thing alone. Visitors enter the grounds through the gift shop to the base of solid stone on which the castle was built.

Then they ascend a narrow spiral staircase into a tower and totter along a walkway around the topmost fortress walls to reach the stone. Brave souls wishing to perform the obligatory ritual must lay on their backs, bend backward, and lean up and under the rampart. Stationed at the stone is a courtly Irish gentleman who holds the legs of men so they don't tumble over the precipice and inadvertently end their Irish vacation several hundred feet below. This same gent also will discreetly drape a blanket over a skirt-wearing woman's knees before grabbing her ankles and whispering words of encouragement.

Having kissed the stone, the smoocher is allegedly blessed with what one visiting eighteenth-century Frenchman impolitely called the "privilege of speaking only lies for the next seven years."

When leaving the castle, after retracing their steps, those who kissed the stone can purchase an official-looking parchment attesting to their new gift of gab. However, there have been several guests who knocked their noggins on that castle wall and could not remember if they lip-surfed the stone or not. If this is the case, the blanket-wielding courtier will, of course, bear witness that the deed was indeed performed in proper form. It's not known whether or not the gentleman himself has kissed storied stone.

♣

## The Way of the Leprecaun

THE LEPRECAUNS HAD ceased to work and were looking at the children. Seumas turned to them.

"God bless the work," said he politely.

One of the Leprecauns, who had a grey, puckered face and a thin fringe of grey whiskers very far under his chin, then spoke.

"Come over here, Seumas Beg," said he, "and I'll measure you for a pair of shoes. Put your foot up on that root."

The boy did so, and the Leprecaun took the measure of his foot with a wooden rule.

"Now, Brigid Beg, show me your foot," and he measured her also. "They'll be ready for you in the morning."

"Do you never do anything else but make shoes, sir?" said Seumas.

"We do not," replied the Leprecaun, "except when we want new clothes, and then we have to make them, but we grudge every minute spent making anything else except shoes, because that is the proper work for a Leprecaun. In the night time we go about the country into people's houses and we clip little pieces off their money, and so, bit by bit, we get a crock of gold together, because, do you see, a Leprecaun has to have a crock of gold so that if he's captured by men folk he may be able to ransom himself. But that seldom happens, because it's a great disgrace altogether to be captured by a man, and we've practised so long dodging among the roots here that we can easily get away from them. Of course, now and again we are caught; but men are fools, and we always escape without having to pay the ransom at all. We wear green clothes because it is the color of grass and the leaves, and when we sit down under a bush or lie in the grass they just walk by without noticing us."

—*JAMES STEPHENS,* THE CROCK OF GOLD

THE LAND of faery,
Where nobody gets old and godly and grave,
Where nobody gets old and crafty and wise,
Where nobody gets old and bitter of tongue.

—*WILLIAM BUTLER YEATS,*
*"LAND OF HEART'S DESIRE"*

IT'S EASY TO halve the potato when there's love.

—*IRISH PROVERB*

# The People of the Auld Sod

IF YOU ARE lucky enough to be Irish, you are lucky enough.

—*IRISH PROVERB*

## On the Road

IRISH "TRAVELERS," or tinkers as they are more commonly known, have a fascinating backround, most of it lost in the dim recesses of history. There are many possible explanations about how these wanderers came to be. But they have been part of the Irish countryside for generations. Their caravans are spotted huddled at the edges of towns or moving slowly along Ireland's narrow roadways.

Some historians think the travelers are descendents of orphaned and abandoned children cast out during the Great Famine of the 1840s. Others suggest that they might have been descendants of Irish families fleeing English general Oliver Cromwell when he invaded the island in the seventeenth century. More likely, it is possible that the travelers are actually descendants of Bronze Age tinsmiths. They may even be related to Europe's nomadic clans, such as gypsies.

In the old days, travelers performed a great service by repairing pots and pans or selling horses and donkeys. Before the age of television and telephone, they carried the latest news from village to village.

Contemporary traveling families now often make their living by recycling scrap, reupholstering furniture, asphalting driveways, and performing other odd jobs. Families are tight-knit, often having ten or more children who help earn money from an early age. The Irish government is encouraging the travelers to settle down and become part of the community. While some have taken advantage of government assistance and now are more or less settled in their homes, they still keep their trailers close at hand in the backyard. Since the call of history is strong, they still spend part of the time on the road.

THE GREAT THING about the Irish is that they generally retain great affection for their homeland. We are a very dispersed people but there is that old longing for the homeland.

—*JOSEPH SMALL, IRISH AMBASSADOR TO GREAT BRITAIN*

## He's Drinking for Two Now

MIKE WALKS INTO a bar in Dublin, orders three pints of Guinness and sits in the back of the room, drinking a sip out of each one in turn. When he finishes them, he comes back to the bar and orders three more.

The bartender asks him, "You know, a pint goes flat after I draw it; it would taste better if you bought one at a time."

Mike replies, "Well, you see, I have two brothers. One is in America, the other in Australia, and I'm here in Dublin. When we all left home, we promised that we'd drink this way to remember the days when we drank together."

Mike becomes a regular in the bar, and always drinks the same way: He orders three pints and drinks them in turn.

One day, he comes in and orders only two pints. All the other regulars notice and fall silent.

When Mike comes back to the bar for the second round, the bartender says, "Please let me offer my condolences on your great loss."

Mike looks confused for a moment, then a light dawns in his eye and he laughs. "Oh, no," he says, "everyone's fine. I've just quit drinking."

WE HAD COMMUNITY. There was no need for psychiatrists or tranquilizers or anything because we had each other.

—*MAISIE FLYNN, ON CORK CITY IN THE 1930S*

IT IS NOT a matter of upper or lower class, but of being up a while and down a while.

—*IRISH PROVERB*

WE ARE A great people for minding everyone else's business.

—*CORK RESIDENT*

YOUR FEET WILL bring you to where your heart is.

—*IRISH PROVERB*

WHAT REALLY FLATTERS a man is that you think him worth flattering.

—*GEORGE BERNARD SHAW,*
JOHN BULL'S OTHER ISLAND

## A Little Milk With Your Latte?

IN IRELAND, COFFEE has always taken a backseat to a good "cuppa" tea. But times change, and even a place as bound to tradition as Ireland is in step with the coffee craze that has swept the States.

For years, a small restaurant in Derry had on its menu a drink called milky coffee. It was in essence a weak cup of coffee brewed in milk rather than water. It had quickly become a boyhood favorite of one young man who grew up in the Maiden City. Heavily accented with brown sugar, the sweet, mild drink had none of the bitterness associated with a strong "cuppa" and was a perfect match for the heavenly cakes served at the restaurant.

On his last return visit, the nostalgic man was grateful to see the restaurant still standing. Elation turned to despair, however, when he asked for a milky coffee.

"'Fraid we don't have that anymore, love," was the waitress's response. "Would you like a cafe latte or cappuccino instead?"

YET SURELY THEY are very valiant and hardie, for the most part great endurers of colde, labor, hunger, and all hardinesse, very active and strong of hand, very swift of foot, very vigilant and circumspect in their enterprises, very present in perils, very great scorners of death.

—*EDMUND SPENSER,* A VIEW OF IRELAND

THE TIME I speak of, our lives were so thronged with small beauties that you wouldn't think 'twas sons an' daughters of the flesh we were, but children of the rainbow dwellin' always in the mornin' of the world!

—*BRYAN MACMAHON,*
CHILDREN OF THE RAINBOW

A man should never be ashamed to own he has been in the wrong, which is but saying, in other words, that he is wiser today than he was yesterday.

—*JONATHAN SWIFT,*
THOUGHTS ON VARIOUS SUBJECTS

## It's a Rooster's Life

IN 1989, WHILE farmers were protesting with their livestock outside the Dail (the Irish parliament), two roosters escaped into nearby St. Stephen's Green park. For some months, they had a contented, but celibate, bachelorhood.

That was changed when someone left three hens in the park overnight. The donor remained anonymous, but "the two cocks seem to be quite happy about it and it is the mating season," said park keeper Pat Waters.

## A Guinness Legacy

THE GUINNESS FAMILY, the noted Irish brewers, regularly contributed to the renovation of St. Patrick's

Cathedral over the years. It is therefore interesting to note that a monument to Sir Benjamin Guinness's daughter stands under a stained glass window bearing the words, "I was thirsty and ye gave me drink."

## Straight Talk

"HOW LONG WILL you be in Ireland?" asked the expatriate American living in Dublin.

"About six months."

"Great!" she said. "That means you'll be around long enough to get a straight answer or two!"

THESE DAYS, and in this traffic, you have to be plenty brave to be a coward.

—*DUBLIN CAB DRIVER*

JAYZUS! ON THE eighth day, Lord God A'mighty musta created those damn bagpipes.

—*PASSERBY COMMENTING ON A SCOTTISH PIPE BAND TUNING UP AT MILWAUKEE IRISH FEST*

## How to Win a Pub

IF THE LIFE of an Irish pub keeper is your idea of heaven, then you'll believe Doug Knight died and went to Tir na nog, the Gaelic afterlife. In 1997, Knight and his wife, Suzanne, were winners in the fourth annual Guinness Imports "Win a Pub" competition. Formerly of Minneapolis, the two are now residents of Cahir, the Crossroads of Munster. Their pub, Morrissey's, is on the main road between Cork and Dublin and across the River Suir from the local castle.

Knight's was one of the 10 qualifying essays out of 50,000-plus entries. He successfully completed the sentence "As the cool, creamy head of a pint of Guinness settles..." with "millions of particles at the subatomic level displaced by pressure variance propelled toward the surface creating this phenomenon serving in the purpose of topping off our subject with just the right amount making scientifically, a perfect pint of stout."

He cheerfully pointed out that his wife actually wrote their response while they were waiting in an auto repair shop for their car to be fixed. They agreed up front to have his name on the entry.

The finalists were flown to Ireland for a last round of activities. They had to place well in dart tossing, pouring a perfect pint, and telling the judges why they deserved to own the place. It helped that Knight, dressed in black throughout the competition, crooned a Van Morrison love tune to the pint he had just poured. The words and music seemed to help settle the foamy head during those much-anticipated seconds—beloved by deliberate thinkers and stout drinkers—commonly known as "Guinness Time."

His final verbal rendition, the one that put him over the top, went like this:

I see myself as publican
It's Morrissey's, by Knight
I'm serving stout and clasping hands
I smell the fresh pub pies
I taste a pint of Guinness or two (or three!)
Hear the fiddler play our song
With all five senses telling me
That Cahir's where I belong!

He immediately announced another round on the house, earning an appreciative roar from those in attendance. Then a Tippperary-tinged voice from the rear of the crowd loudly reminded the new publican that it was his turn that night to clean up.

♣

## A Pub Keeper's Tale

FINNEGAN THE PUB KEEPER was carefully mopping up the bar counter and chatting with Sullivan, Flaherty, and O'Malley. Narrow shafts of afternoon sunlight danced across the mirror in back and bounced off the deep, dark amber liquid in the men's glasses. Ah, it was a grand afternoon, they all agreed.

"Would you believe it?," Finnegan asks the three, pausing in his task.

They look puzzled. "Tell us more," Sullivan replies, sensing a good story. Flaherty and O'Malley lean over their drinks, elbows on the bar. Ready for anything, they are.

"Well, last night, I heard this tremendous racket down here in the pub. I roll over in me bed and I tell Herself, 'Now who could that be at this time o' night.' She shivers and pulls the covers over her head, 'Wisha! Could it be a burglar? Maybe a pooka? Lord have mercy on us all!' she says, making the sign of the cross," Finnegan relates.

His listeners are really tuned in by this time.

"So I pick me blackthorn cane, ye know the one I carry to rap on the likes o' ye fellows when ye get outta hand," he nods to the stout stick standing at attention behind the bar. "So, I creep down the stairs and peer out from behind the door there.

"I musta spilled a drop or two o' Guinness on the floor as I was closing up last night. And in the middle of the puddle was this wee brown mouse. Right fine in his cups he was, making all sorts o' rarin' sound, jumpin' around on his hind legs and boxin' with his paws for all the world like the great John L. Sulllivan himself. A fine broth of a mouse, he was," Finnegan goes on. "And ye know what he was rarin', boys?"

They shook their heads.

"He was yellin' out, 'Bring on the cat! Bring on the cat!'"

WHAT I ESPECIALLY like about Englishmen is that, after they have called you a thief and a liar and have patted you on the back for being so charming in spite of it, they look honestly depressed if you fail to see that they have been paying you a handsome compliment.

—*ROBERT LYND*

## A New World Success Story

ONE HUNDRED YEARS of service in the legal profession was celebrated in 1996 at the McGlynn & McGlynn law firm in Belleview, Illinois, across the muddy Mississippi River from St. Louis. Family patriarch Daniel Francis McGlynn, founder of the firm, hung out his shingle in 1896. He was born in Illinois of Irish parents, but had returned to the home island to find his bride. He brought back a lovely wife and her entire family, including mom, dad, and ten siblings.

An outspoken advocate of the Church, McGlynn declared that his boys should go to the University of Notre Dame, setting a precedent that would draw 26 McGlynn descendants to the university.

The elder McGlynn was a practicing lawyer at the turn of the century when the pastor of his St. Patrick's Church died, leaving numerous Irish parishioners to wonder who would be assigned as their priest. A German priest was eventually named, to the alarm of the congregation. This just shouldn't be! The people did not accept the new clergyman and even barred him from entering St. Patrick's.

The local bishop threatened everyone involved with excommunication and a stand-off resulted. Old Dan knew, as the family story goes, "a wee bit o' canon law." So he countered that the parishioners had the right to approve who could serve them. Then, knowing that the papal nuncio was going to be visiting Notre Dame at the time, McGlynn took the train to South Bend, Indiana, the university's home. He told the parish's story to the pope's representative and, ultimately, an Irish priest was named as pastor.

There have been 14 lawyers in the McGlynn family since that time. In the 1990s, one of the contemporary McGlynns, Joseph B. Jr., was honorary Irish consul in St. Louis.

NATURE DID ME that honour.

—*DION LARDNER BOUCICAULT, WHEN ASKED IF HE WAS AN IRISHMAN*

MY ONE CLAIM to originality among Irishmen is that I have never made a speech.

—*GEORGE MOORE, IRISH AUTHOR*

NO MAN EVER gave advice
but himself were the better for it.

—*IRISH PROVERB*

## An Otherworldly Encounter

WELL-KNOWN WISCONSIN land developer Gordon Russell was about to visit Ireland a few years ago. Prior to his adventure, he thumbed through the family album, where the Russell likeness was obvious in almost every photograph. Two generations previously, a number of the Russell brothers—including Gordon's grandfather and several great-uncles—had emigrated to America. Two others stayed behind at the farm in Templemore, County Tipperary. They passed the old homestead on to their descendants while the American side of the clan also prospered and expanded.

Upon his arrival in the Auld Sod, Gordon dropped by the old family farm to say hello to Jimmie, Johnnie, and Mary. Then in their late sixties, the two brothers and their sister had never married and were the sole surviving Russells living on the place. When he walked up the path to the cottage, he saw Mary in

the back, pulling weeds from her expansive flower and vegetable garden.

Hoping not to startle her, Gordon offered a cheery hello. Mary straightened, turned around, and screamed. She threw her apron over her head and said, "Glory be to God, it's my father come back from the dead!"

It took a bit to settle everyone down after that. But it was certainly a quick and ready way to break the ice. Naturally, the subsequent chat focused on all the Russells and what each side of the family was doing. And throughout Gordon's visit, Mary kept shaking her head over the family look-alikes.

HILLS AS GREEN as emeralds
Cover the countryside
Lakes as blue as sapphires—
Are Ireland's special pride
And rivers that shine like silver
Make Ireland look so fair—
But the friendliness of her people
Is the richest treasure there.

—*IRISH BLESSING*

## New World Meets the Old

PRESIDENT JOHN F. KENNEDY was always openly welcomed and almost revered by the Irish. Everyone in the country felt they had a bit of ownership in the good-looking, vibrant young Irish-American leader. Here is one such statement of adulation:

"We, the women of Limerick and county, feel we have a special claim on you: We claim the Fitzgeralds. May I repeat, we claim the Fitzgerald in you, Sir, and we are extremely proud of that heritage," said Lady Mayoress Frances Condell, lady mayoress of Limerick, speaking to Kennedy when he visited Limerick in 1963.

"Over there, you see a large number of your relatives and connections who have come to greet you on the distaff side. As a matter of fact, there is only one Kennedy amongst them, a man named Padraig, who has actually written a history, an American history, and who quoted and forecasted many years ago that you would become the President of the United States," she added, pointing to the crowd of well-wishers who had turned out to greet "their own."

"And these good people have come to show our Limerick claim on you, and by their presence they prove that the Fitzgeralds are proud of their own Rose [Kennedy's mother], and her dynamic father,

Honey Fitz, your reputable and thoughtful and most successful grandfather," she went on, much to Kennedy's delight.

## Irish Facts

IRELAND HAS 32 counties, 26 of which are in the Republic of Ireland (the south) and six of which make up Northern Ireland. The major cities are Dublin, Belfast, Cork, Derry, Galway, and Limerick. The population of Ireland is about 5.1 million (1997), with one-third of the total living in the urban areas.

THE HOSPITALITY OF an Irishman is not the running account of posted and ledgered courtesies, as in other countries; it springs, like all his qualities, his faults, his virtues, directly from his heart.

—*DANIEL O'CONNELL, SPEECH AGAINST MARQUESS OF HEADFORT, JULY 1904*

THERE'S MANY A dry eye at a moneylender's funeral.

—*A CORK RESIDENT*

## That's a Lot of Bull!

IT'S NOT THAT Pat and Mary Hanrahan throw a lot of bull, but there is a herd of American bison in the front yard of their farm home just south of Kewaunee, Wisconsin. Hanrahan must be one of the few Irish buffalo breeders in the world, having traded in his dairy cows to raise the woolly critters for beef and hides.

Spike, a buffalo bull who meandered away from the herd a year or so ago, literally hangs out in the family dining room. Or rather, a third of Spike—the front third—hangs out. The old boy had to be put down because of his wandering tendencies (it's hard to argue with almost a ton-plus of meandering beef). The head was mounted and hung on the wall, a trophy that now occupies a place of honor just behind Hanrahan's right shoulder when he sits down for supper. Mary assures visitors that, no, the other part of Spike is not on the opposite side of the wall.

## The Couple

AH, MOLLY
an eye on the turf fire
setting the pot to boil
You're waiting for him to return
up from the bogland
damp with the fever of work
You and the Man
lean boned, muscled, gnarled of hand
yet always together
Ah, Molly
eye toward the door
waiting for the King of Limerick
Hard by the rookery
where the great birds play
you and he whistle a wind song

—*MARTIN RUSSELL*

SIR KNIGHT! I feel not the least alarm;
No son of Erin will offer me harm;
For tho' they love woman and golden store,
Sir Knight, they love honour and virtue more!

—*THOMAS MOORE, "RICH AND RARE"*

## Matchmaker, Matchmaker...

Forget the personals. Scrap the video matchmaking service. Don't even bother with the *Dating Game*. If it's a mate you're after, get thee-self off to Lisdoonvarna.

This tiny town of fewer than one thousand souls on the western coast of Ireland, near the otherworldly, desolate Burren, is host to an annual matchmaking fair that draws tens of thousands of lovelorn people each September.

The International Matchmaking Fair, as it's officially called these days, has rather humble roots. This has always been a rural, hard land, farmed by fiercely independent folk who were kept busy from sunup to sundown during the growing season. With the harvest safely completed, families headed to the nearest town for a bit of unwinding. For many young singles, the frequent post-harvest dances in towns like Lisdoonvarna were the most important social occasions of the year—and most certainly offered the best chances to meet other eligible young folk of the opposite sex.

Around the turn of the century, some of the area's wealthier families began relying upon the Lisdoonvarna "fairs" to select suitable mates for their children and even to plan arranged marriages.

The town's matchmaking reputation quickly spread. Soon, lonely hearts from throughout Ireland began checking into Lisdoonvarna's heartbreak hotels each autumn. The townspeople say the matchmaking festivals have resulted in hundreds of marriages over the years. Bear in mind, of course, that the annual influx of the lovesick has been a boon to this tiny town.

So, does your mate await you in Lisdoonvarna? Who knows. But you could do worse than spend a few autumn days among the friendly folks there.

I LIVE IN Ireland by choice, after experience of living in many other places, and I am happy here. Our neighbours are friendly, our view is beautiful, my political friends are fine upstanding people, my political enemies fascinating in their own way. I don't mind the gossip any more than the rain. The censors are no longer eating writers in the street. We are not as bad as we are painted, especially by ourselves. In fact, I love Ireland, as most Irish people do, with only an occasional fit of the shudders.

—*CONOR CRUISE O'BRIEN,* STATES OF IRELAND

## The Ultimate Toast

IN 1997, 50,238 drinkers across the United States simultaneously lifted their pints in celebration of the Great Irish Toast. The aim was to set a new world record in toasting for inclusion in the *Guinness Book of World Records*. After a lengthy review process, the number was duly noted by the record book.

Hundreds of bars and restaurants in 30 cities nationwide took part in the fourth annual and biggest-ever Guinness toast. Official brewery representatives were on hand at all participating locations to register "toasters" and provide the proper documentation for entry into the world's most famous book of facts.

Guinness remains the best selling stout in the United States, with all its tap product coming directly from its St. James's Gate Brewery in Dublin.

IN THE GREATER part of Ireland, however,
the whole people, from the tinkers to the clergy,
have still a life, and a view of life,
that are rich and genial and humorous.

—*JOHN MILLINGTON SYNGE,*
THE TINKER'S WEDDING

THE BRAINS AND tongues of the Irish are somehow differently formed or furnished from those of other people.

—*SIR JONAH BARRINGTON,* PERSONAL SKETCHES

I HAVE BEEN three years in this country (Ireland)
and never found a dull man.

—*LADY RANDOLPH,*
*MOTHER OF WINSTON CHURCHILL*

MAY THE HINGES of our friendship
never grow rusty.

—*OLD IRISH TOAST*

## A Comfy Wrap

THE HEAVY SHAWL was a staple item of clothing for Irish women for generations. The shawls were usually black, but wearing a dark green one was always considered a step up the social ladder. A special kind of shawl was the "double decker," with so much wool in it there was an extra fold.

The older women were even called "shawlies" because they were never seen without their shawl. They did everything in them, from carrying food to keeping warm. They even used the shawl as a weapon; they could snap one like a whip, and youngsters would think twice about acting up if they had once been caught by a snap.

The women transported infants in their shawls, carrying the babies around in the warm, snug darkness. The shawlies always said this was good for the health of the child. And why not? The baby was comfortable and cozy inside. It was a wonderful way to start life.

LONG LIVE the Irish!
Long live their cheer!
Long live our friendship
Year after year!

*—OLD IRISH TOAST*

MAY THE LILT of Irish laughter
Lighten every load,
May the mist of Irish magic
Shorten every road,
May you taste the sweetest pleasures
That fortune ere bestowed,
And may all your friends remember
All the favors you are owed.

*—IRISH BLESSING*

HERE'S THAT WE may always have
A clean shirt
A clean conscience
And a guinea in our pocket.

*—IRISH BLESSING*

## Not Quite Natural Causes

LOCAL IRISH COURTS offer some of the most endearing and bizarre stories to come out of the Emerald Isle. Once, a farmer sued the local authorities for destroying his cow because of the suspicion that the animal had rabies. If the cow was killed only upon a suspicion, then the farmer would be paid. But if the cow had proved rabid before its destruction, then no payment would be made. The proof usually required a microscopic examination of the spinal cord. However, in this case, no such examination had been performed.

The defense appeared hopeless. But the authorities produced their own doctor, who swore, "That cow had rabies by the infallible test."

"What test did you apply?" asked the magistrate.

"Brought a dog into the stall with the cow and the cow begins to bark—that's the only infallible test."

The judge doubted the doctor's medical ability and asked, "Was that the only symptom you noticed in this case?"

The doctor did not hesitate. "No, in this case, there was the sudden death of the cow."

"Hmmm," said the judge. "Did she die very suddenly?"

"Very suddenly," said the doctor.

"Described what happened," said the judge.

"I shot her," said the doctor.

## What's in a Name?

MICHAEL VERDON, in his book *Old Cork Remembered,* wrote that the residents of the town were great for handing out nicknames. Everyone seemed to have a moniker. There was one fellow who always ate fast. He was tagged "Murder the Loaf." A tall man was called "Hand Me Down Moon." One moneylender was noted for his tenacity. He would keep coming back to a house until he collected. The folks called him "Dickey Glue" because he stuck to them until he got his money.

WHERE WOULD THE Irish be
without someone to be Irish at?

—*ELIZABETH BOWEN,* THE HOUSE IN PARIS

WE HAVE ALWAYS found the Irish a bit odd.
They refuse to be English.

—*WINSTON CHURCHILL*

THERE WAS ONCE a man who had a beautiful daughter, and many men were in love with her. Among them were two lads who came courting. One of them pleased her; the other did not. The youth she disliked was very rich. He visited her father's house often, just to see the lass and to be in her company. But the fellow she liked was very poor, and he came but seldom.

The girl's father preferred that she marry the rich boy who constantly came to see her. In an effort to advance the fellow's good cause, the father arranged a lavish dinner party and sent everyone in the village an invitation.

"Drink a drink now," says he to his daughter, "on the man you like best in this company." He waited with a smile on his face, thinking she would drink a toast to the man he liked best himself.

She lifted the glass in her hand, stood up, looked round, and then recited:

"I drink the good health of Often-Who-Came,
But who often comes not I also must name;
Who often comes not I often must blame
That he comes not as often as Often-Who-Came."

She sat down when she had spoken her quatrain and said not another word that evening. But the rich youth, Often-Who-Came, understood that it was not he whom the lass wanted, and he did not visit her again. So, with her father's consent, she married the poor but honest man of her choice, and forever after she lived to regret it.

—OFTEN-WHO-CAME, *FOURTH OR FIFTH CENTURY, TRANSLATED BY* D.J. O'DONOGHUE, *1894*

MAY THE ROOF above us never fall in, and may we friends gathered below never fall out.

—*IRISH TOAST*

A PEOPLE [the Irish] so individual in its genius, so tenacious in love or hate, so captivating in its nobler moods.

—*FREDERICK EDWIN SMITH, EARL OF BIRKENHEAD, SPEECH ON IRISH TREATY, HOUSE OF LORDS, 1920*

YOU'RE AN IRISH summer of a man: sunny skies one day and rain the next. For a week or maybe a month you'd be the height of company: you'd make a cat laugh; next thing, there's a face on you like a plateful of mortal sins and you're off out that door as if there was a curtain rod stuck up you. You can get on with no one: a cup of cold water would disagree with you.

—*HUGH LEONARD,* A LIFE

IF ONE COULD only teach the English how to talk and the Irish how to listen, society would be quite civilized.

—*OSCAR WILDE*

THAT'S THE IRISH people all over—they treat a joke as a serious thing and a serious thing as a joke.

—*SEAN O'CASEY*

LET YOUR ANGER set with the sun and not rise again with it.

—*IRISH PROVERB*

THE REASONABLE MAN adapts himself to the world: the unreasonable one persists in trying to adapt the world to himself. Therefore all progress depends on the unreasonable man.

—*GEORGE BERNARD SHAW, "REASON"*

WISDOM MAKES a poor man a king.

—*IRISH PROVERB*

THE IRISH HAVE captured the world's imagination, and the game of interpreting them has been going on for centuries, often with doubtful results.

—*ANONYMOUS*

O' LOVE IS THE soul of a true Irishman;
He loves all that's lovely, loves all that he can,
With his sprig of shillelagh and shamrock so green.

—*"SPRIG OF SHILLELAGH," ATTRIBUTED TO LYSAGHT*

# Religion, Politics, and Other Irish Sports

IN IRELAND the inevitable
never happens and the
unexpected constantly occurs.
—*SIR JOHN PENTLAND MAHAFFY*

## The Perfect Nest

THERE IS A little hollowed place in the cliffs that rise above the upper lakes at Glendalough in the Wicklow Mountains. This is St. Kevin's cell, where the famous saint would remove himself from the world during Lent. The cell was so small that when Kevin praised God every morning, he had to stick one arm out of the window. Kevin was at such prayer one day, with his arm and hand stretched outside, when a blackbird landed on his hand.

She settled herself and, as St. Kevin liked a little animal company, he went on with his prayers. But the bird found the hand comfortable. She therefore laid an egg in Kevin's open hand. So what should good saint do in such a predicament? He remained kneeling, his arm extended and his hand opened, until the egg hatched and the fledgling was old enough to fly.

## Hey, It's Only a Game!

NEVER DOUBT THAT the Irish are passionate about soccer, which they know as "football." *Irish Voice* sports reporter Liam Hayes caught the tone of preliminary World Cup fever in a column dated November 17, 1992. He wrote excitedly, with a bit o' tongue in cheek, about the Irish soccer team's perceived capabilities against their Spanish rivals in a qualifying match.

"Hell, the Spaniards don't stand a snowball's chance in Ramon Sanchez Pizjuan's backyard! They're inexperienced compared to us, and their new manager Javier Clemente hasn't even built a reliable team for himself yet. Wait until McGrath starts marching through them, Houghton gets down to clipping their heels, and Quinn starts throwing those long arms and legs of his about. Pressure? They'll melt in their own kitchen!

"And who has ever beaten Jack [Irish coach Jack Charlton] and the lads at their own game?

"Yes, the answer is nobody. Okay, Wales did it twice, and Egypt almost did it in the last World Cup, but who else? Yes, nobody. . . .

"We'll win! And why not?"

The Irish did go on to the next round in the Cup preliminary matches, much to the delight of their fans.

♣

## St. Declan's Bell

The Duiblin Declain is St. Declan's little black bell, which he received from heaven after meeting St. Patrick on a pilgrimage to Rome. The bell did marvelous things. When Declan was trying to return to Ireland from Gaul, no ship could be found to transport him. Declan rang his little bell, and immediately a ship appeared on raging sea. However, when the holy man boarded the vessel, he forgot his bell, leaving it behind on a rock. But Declan offered up a prayer, and the rock floated out to sea. It kept pace with his ship for the entire voyage. When the ship and its crew reached the Irish shore, the rock and the bell sped ahead to a nearby spit of land.

Declan landed at the hallowed spot and founded his church there, at Ardmore in County Waterford.

## Let's Give Him a Hand

St. Aengus of Laois lived with the wild animals as a hermit before joining a monastery at Clonenagh. When living as a monk, he volunteered for the most menial chores. One day, St. Aengus found himself at one of these tasks, chopping wood. Unfortunately, his axe slipped, and off went the saint's left hand.

Immediately, St. Aengus was surrounded by birds, all crying out in pain. But Aengus remained confident in the goodness of God. He merely picked up his severed hand and put it back on his arm. The hand was instantly reattached and the good saint continued his chores. The less reverent of the Irish ever afterwards have said that St. Aengus was something of a cutup.

IRISH PEOPLE ARE interested in politics, any old dog fight at all. Irish people are opinionated and like to debate their opinions. They would love to argue over a two-penny piece.

—*EDMUND O'CALLAGHAN, CELBRIDGE, COUNTY CLARE*

THERE SHOULD be more female presidents.

—*CHICAGOAN CHARI MCNALLY AT A RECEPTION FOR IRISH PRESIDENT MARY ROBINSON*

## Can't Top That One!

**M**ARATHON CYCLIST Pat Kerrigan had a tinker's bag full of adventures during one ride around the rim of Ireland. During a stop in a pub at Ballybunion, County Kerry, he listened to a conversation among 13 or 14 patrons arguing in the middle of the afternoon about who poured the best pint of Guinness.

"A couple of the guys were fishermen, from what they were saying," Kerrigan recalled. "All of a sudden, one of them reaches into a bag and pulls out this big fish, a turbot, I think it was, and said he was taking it home to his mother. That ended the conversation!"

**M**AY THERE always be work for your hands to do...
May your purse always hold a coin or two...
May the sun always shine on your windowpane.
May a rainbow be certain to follow each rain...
May the hand of a friend always be near you.

May God fill your heart with gladness to cheer you.
And, until we meet again,
May God hold you in the palm of his hand.

—*IRISH BLESSING*

## Another Animal Story

ST. MULLEN OF Carlow loved animals so much that he not only rescued a wren that had been swallowed by a cat, but also rescued a fly that had been swallowed by the wren.

## A Tale of Adventure

THE FANTASTIC VOYAGE of the Irish holy man St. Brendan to America in the sixth century, almost one thousand years before Columbus set sail, was one of the most popular books of the Middle Ages.

## The Real Story on Saints

THERE ARE HUNDREDS of Irish saints, both male and female. But only three have been officially canonized by the Catholic Church: Malachy, Laurence O'Toole, and Oliver Plunkett.

## Fun on the Skelligs

IN THE WEST of Ireland, off the coast of Kerry, there lies a desolate group of islands known as the Skellig Rocks. In ancient times, an unknown race of people lived in tiny cells on the islands, made up of rocks fitted upon other rocks. When the Church came to the islands, the monks used the cells to retire for silence and prayer. But they, too, eventually abandoned the place to the raucous seabirds.

Eventually, there arose a custom among the young people of Kerry called "going to the Skelligs." Back then, marriages were not allowed from February to April during Lent, the religious season when Catholics fast and pray. So young Irish couples, being enterprising, started to make a pilgrimage to the Skellig Rocks during the last week of Lent. The stated purpose of this journey was to spend the week in the rock cells in prayer—the women prayed for good husbands while the men repented their sins. Tar barrels were even brought over to the islands to be lighted as guides for the young people as they traversed the dangerous rocky paths of their penance.

However, things being what they were even back then, good intentions soon dissolved into a mad carnival of dancing, drinking, and general fun. The priests denounced the practice of sailing out to the

Skelligs and declared the islands closed. But the practice continued for years until the police cleared the rocky outcroppings and prevented any youthful landings. Now only the birds and the occasional tourist are allowed to cross the choppy waters to have fun on the Skelligs.

THERE IS NOTHING the Irish like better than a good political row. And it doesn't seem to matter whose row it is. We will haggle over a fine point of political rhetoric as happily as the rights and wrongs of the price of rice in Sierra Leone. And you can bet your bottom dollar there will be enough participants on both sides of the argument to keep it going for weeks.

—*DICK AHLSTROM, DEPUTY NEWS EDITOR,* THE IRISH TIMES

ENGLAND AND IRELAND may flourish together. The world is large enough for us both. Let it be our care not to make ourselves too little for it.

—*EDMUND BURKE,* LETTER TO SAMUEL SPAN

## So, Where Are the Pins?

YANKS DRIVING IN Ireland have plenty to think about. There's the whole bit about being on the wrong side of the road that takes most of the average holiday stay to sort out. Then there's the incredibly narrow roads to get used to. They are lanes really, which offer next to no passing room. Sheep are everywhere as well; a mutton chop may be sunning itself on the asphalt just around the next bend. This can all be a little overwhelming, really.

Which is why easily rattled motorists will stay off the roads in Armagh and Cork counties on Sundays. It's not the spiritually enlightened folk coming and going to church that's the worry, it's the bowlers.

Road bowling is an immensely popular sport in parts of Ireland. Bunches of grown men will spend

the better part of a Sunday flinging wee balls down mile after mile of country lanes. It may seem more like the pastime of a group of bored teenagers and it may be hard to imagine there being much draw to it at all. Skeptical tourists, in fact, might wonder if the whole thing isn't just one huge inside joke being played on naive visitors. But one visit to a road bowling match ought to convince even the most unbelieving that this sport is for real.

Hundreds of spectators often line the roadsides for the matches, in which two players vie to complete the several-mile course in the fewest number of throws, all while keeping the bowling ball, a cast iron sphere weighing upwards of 28 ounces, from straying off the road.

If you do venture out onto the roadways of Cork or Armagh on a fair Sunday afternoon, don't bother looking for blimps or kids wearing T-shirts screaming "Just Threw It"; this is a strictly amateur sport (though it's been rumored a bit of wagered money may change hands during the course of the day). Do, however, keep a sharp eye out for that little iron ball. It'll likely be quickly followed by a frenetic man in the throes of a fit of body English. Or is that body Irish?

☘

## A Special Club

AVID GOLFER Alex McGrath of Chicago's Donegal Imports usually takes to the links before the last snow melts from the greens of his closest club. Ever a duffer, McGrath once displayed an Irish-made shillelagh-style putter in his shop window. It barely had a chance to gather a speck o' dust before it was purchased by Mark Howard, head of the noted Trinity Irish Dance Company, who was on his way to New York to appear on the Jay Leno St. Patrick's Day television show. Howard then presented Leno with the golf club, much to the TV host's appreciation.

THE WORLD WOULD not make
a racehorse of a donkey.

—*IRISH PROVERB*

WHEN YOUR HAND is in the dog's mouth,
withdraw it gently.

—*IRISH PROVERB*

## Race Day

THE CROSS CARRIED its message across
the winding path, down from the steeple,
where not many really listened
Because it was race day at Fairyhouse
All the Meath men were betting
heavy coins in stained hands,
placing their hopes on Dougan's little mare
No need for church bells today
Yet the way the race ended
there should have been more prayers
from the congregation, rain-soaked
The gelding named Joseph won

—*MARTIN RUSSELL*

AN IRISHMAN WILL bet on a fly
crawling up a wall.

—*GALWAY TURF ACCOUNTANT (BOOKIE)*

LIFE IS MUCH too important a thing ever to talk
seriously about it.

—*OSCAR WILDE,* VERA, OR THE NIHILISTS

## Finicky Fish

AN AMERICAN VISITOR was anxious to sample the fighting abilities of the wild Irish trout. He brought his prize fly rod and picked his best trout flies. He booked a room at a farm along the River Suir, one of Ireland's best fishing waterways. The Yank carefully studied the river's riffles and pools to learn where the trout lived. He waited for dusk, for the trout would only rise with the coming of the moon.

Careful planning paid off. He heard the splash of a rising trout and he tried his best fly first. It bobbed merrily along the water, but not a fish looked at it. He tried other flies. No bites. He went to the pools and cast again. Still no trout expressed anything but disdain for his flies.

He returned the next night and again not a bite. Even the wonders of the fresh outside and the magical hills of Ireland were losing their allure. But being a fisherman means that every tomorrow is a new day. So the American was back out on the river on his last night. He was almost at the point of resorting to prayer when an elderly lady with a long pole appeared on the other side of the river.

"Much luck?" she asked.

"Nothing," the American grumbled. "I don't think these are even trout. They won't bite at anything."

"And what are you using?" asked the old woman. The American named all of his flies, the Blue Dun, the Royal Coachman, the Olive-Winged Mayfly. In desperation, he'd even tried an old Mosquito fly. With this, the woman burst into laughter.

"Sure, those are American bugs," she said. "These fish have never even seen a Mosquito. Just like most folks around here, they're a bit thickheaded. They only know Irish bugs."

Then she cast an old piece of string into the water. On its end was tied a bit of clear fishing line and a small black gnat. A 15-inch trout rose and took it up in an instant. As the elderly lady pulled in her trophy, the American swore he'd never fish again . . .

. . . until his next trip to Ireland.

MAY THE LORD keep you in His hand
And never close His fist too tight on you.

—*IRISH BLESSING*

## Pointing to Eternity

A CLAREMAN FOND of hunting was proud of the new setter he had just purchased. The dog had come from the purest stock and was rumored to be almost magical in its ability to find game and stay on point. It was a grand dog, everyone agreed. As the talk progressed, the expected qualities of the animal grew and grew and grew.

As soon as the weather permitted, the man invited his neighbors on a hunt with his new setter in order to show off the dog's marvelous talents. As the group trod out to the wild, windblown cliffs of Clare, the dog suddenly disappeared into the brush. It was close to the end of spring and the leaves were full and green.

No one could see the dog and, call as he might, the worried owner could not get the setter to come. The man and many of his friends searched all day but could not find the dog.

Finally, his friends persuaded the man that the dog, unfamiliar with the lay of the land, had gotten lost and fallen off a steep cliff into the raging sea. The man was distraught, for not only had he lost a fine hunting dog, but he also felt like a fool.

Summer passed, the dog was forgotten, and the cold breezes of autumn blew off the leaves from the bushes. And the man was out on the cliffs again, dreaming of the next year's hunt.

As he was strolling along, he came upon the spot where the setter had disappeared. In the tangle of the brush, now bereft of its leafy cover, the man saw two skeletons. One was the setter, still in a perfect set, his tail bones erect and his nose bone pointed deeper into the brush. For that is where the skeleton of a pheasant stood, still frozen . . . evading the hunters.

MAY THE ROAD rise to meet you.
May the wind be always at your back.
May the sun shine warm upon your face;
The rains fall soft upon your fields
And, until we meet again,
May God hold you in the palm of His hand.

—*GAELIC BLESSING*

## Great Irish Pastime–Hurling

HURLING IS OFTEN considered the national sport of Ireland. A cross between field hockey, soccer, and general mayhem, the game is played with a wooden stick shaped like a broad scythe and a ball about the same size and consistency as a baseball. The object is to send the ball into a goal or through the uprights. If neither of these is possible, then settling for injuring as many opposing team members as possible is acceptable.

The tradition of hurling matches pitting county against county and town against town is centuries old. Such matches were considered high festivals. The prettiest girl in the village was chosen as the hurling queen. Dressed in a white gown that was passed on from queen to queen, the girl led a procession of young women, pipers, and fiddlers to the hurling field.

There they were met by a procession of the young men from the village led by the chief hurler, who was always a well-formed youth at least six feet tall. Then the chief hurler and the hurling queen would join hands and began to dance amid the cheers of the crowd.

After the opening of the hurling, the match would immediately commence and all thoughts of festivities would end as the teams got down to the serious business of beating each other's brains out. The matches were extraordinarily violent. Some were known to have lasted for days and to have spread across the countryside with one side following the ball into another county.

But once the match had finished, the festival began again with a great supper of food, drink, and dancing. This, of course, was followed by much romance and, later, by many marriages between the young people of neighboring villages. Thus did hurling help ensure that villages would never make actual war upon each other.

Today, of course, hurling is much more "refined." The Gaelic Athletic Association governs the sport and makes certain that the rules are followed. However, the ferocity of hurling remains. "The clash of the ash," nicknamed after the hurley, or ash stick, is one of the most popular games played in Ireland.

**A** WELL-TIED TIE is the first serious step in life.

—*OSCAR WILDE,* THE IMPORTANCE OF BEING EARNEST

## Saintly Origins

ST. PATRICK IS not actually Irish by birth. He was the son of a Christian official who lived on the western shores of Roman Britain in the late fourth century. When Patrick was 16, he was captured by an Irish raiding party and taken back to Ireland to be sold as a slave. Patrick was bought by one of the local kings and for six years he tended sheep for his master in the Slemish mountains of County Antrim in the north.

When he was 22, an angel appeared to him and told him to escape. Patrick ran off, made his way to the coast, and stowed away on a ship bound for France. Patrick remained in France for eight years, studying in the local monastery, until one night, the same angel appeared to him again.

As Patrick related in his *Confessions,* "I saw in a dream a man called Victor who seemed to be from Ireland and had many letters. He gave me one and I read the opening words, The Voice of the Irish. And as I read the beginning, I seemed at that moment to hear the voice of those people. They cried as with one voice: 'We beg you, holy youth, come and walk once more among us.'"

Patrick revealed his dream to the local archbishop, and soon he was commissioned by the Pope to set out on his mission to convert the Irish.

Legend has it that St. Patrick's first act was to challenge the local Druidic priests. He traveled to the land surrounding Tara, the home of the pagan high kings and priests. As the Druids prepared to light their fires to celebrate the coming of the spring, Patrick went to the top of the Hill of Slane and lit the Easter fire.

The Druids seized him and took him before Laoghire, the pagan king. The priests told Laoghire that they would show him that Patrick and his religion were not as powerful as the Druids by killing Patrick with a cup of wine laced with poison. But an angel revealed the poison to Patrick. Then he boldly took the cup, said a blessing over it, and drank it to the bottom. When Patrick did not die but asked for more wine, Laoghire was astounded. He accepted Christianity, and his whole court followed suit; Patrick's mission had begun.

☘

## Presidential Connections

TWENTY American presidents can claim some Irish connection. They include John Adams, second president (1791-1801), with ancestral roots in Ulster; James Monroe, fifth president (1816-1820), Derry; John Quincy Adams, sixth president (1825-1829), son of John Adams; Andrew Jackson, seventh president (1829-1837), County Antrim; James Polk, eleventh president (1845-1849), Derry; James Buchanan, fifteenth president (1857-1861), County Donegal; Andrew Johnson, seventeenth president (1865-1869), Ulster; Ulysses S. Grant, eighteenth president (1869-1877), County Tyrone; Chester Alan Arthur, twenty-first president (1881-1885), County Antrim; Grover Cleveland, twenty-second and twenty-fourth president (1885-1889 and 1893-1897), Ulster; William McKinley, twenty-fifth president (1897-1901), County Antrim; William Howard Taft, twenty-seventh president (1909-1913), southern Ireland; Woodrow Wilson, twenty-eighth president (1913-1921), County Tyrone; Warren Harding, twenty-ninth president (1921-1923), southern Ireland; Herbert Hoover, thirty-first president (1929-1933), Ireland; Harry S Truman, thirty-third president (1945-1953), Ireland; John Fitzgerald Kennedy, thirty-fifth president (1961-1963), Wexford; Richard Nixon, thirty-seventh president (1969-1974), Kildare and Laois; Ronald Reagan, fortieth president (1980-1988), County Tipperary; Bill Clinton, forty-second president (1992-2000), County Fermanagh.

## A Dragon's Grave

IRELAND HAS FEW loughs, or lakes, more picturesque than Gougane Barra, Gaelic for "St. Finbar's Rock Cleft," near the headwaters of the River Lee in County Cork. It is surrounded by rugged mountains and fed by a freshwater stream through a rocky gap on its course to Lough Allua. In the center of the peaceful lake is a small island with the ruins of a shrine, which was once the scene of many pilgrimages in old Ireland.

It is said that St. Finbar, under St. Patrick's direction, drowned a murderous dragon in the lake. Supposedly, Patrick had missed driving out this monster when he chased the other reptiles from the island. St. Finbar was then told to build a chapel near where he slaughtered the beast. He moved onto the island to live, and the many ruins dotting the point of land were places where he supposedly slept . . . when they were in better shape, of course.

## Old St. Patrick's Traditions

ST. PATRICK'S DAY is one of Ireland's most important festivals; however, until recently, it was considered a religious holiday rather than one for parades and parties as in the United States. One of the first mentions of the Irish wearing a symbol in honor of St. Patrick's Day was in 1681. English traveler Thomas Dinely wrote the following in his journal. Please note the spellings!

"The 17th day of March yeerly is St. Patrick's, an immovable feast when the Irish of all stations and condicions wore crosses in their hats, some of pins, some of green ribbon, and the vulgar superstitiously wear shamroges, three-leaved grass, which they likewise eat (they say) to cause a sweet breath. The common people and the servants also demand their Patrick's groat of their masters, which they goe expressly to town, though half a dozen miles off, to spend, where sometimes it amounts to a piece of eight or a cobb a piece, and few of the zealous are found sober at night."

## A Hunting Tale

AN IRISHMAN TOOK a young visitor from America hunting for geese on the marsh. But the fog was so thick that morning they couldn't see the end of the gun. It was very frustrating because they could hear the geese honking and rising and flying about over their heads. The mist, however, hid the birds from view.

The Irishman thought it would be a shame for the young man to return without having even fired a shot in Ireland. So he told him that the next time they heard the geese rise and honk to fire a blind shot into the fog. The young man did as he was told and a fox fell out of the sky. At a loss to explain this odd happening, the quick-witted Irishman told to his friend that the fog was so thick the fox was walking on it to reach the geese.

ANYONE ACQUAINTED with Ireland knows that the morning of St. Patrick's Day consists of the night of the 17th of March, flavoured strongly with the morning of the 18th.

—*BALLYHOOLEY (ROBERT J. MARTIN), "ST. PATRICK'S DAY IN THE MORNING"*

## An Irish Farewell

JACKIE CHARLTON, the famed English soccer player and coach, led the Irish team to the international World Cup championship in 1994. Although the team was eventually edged out of the matches, the Irish still praised Charlton for his skill, nicknaming him "Saint Jack." Charlton managed the team from 1986 to 1995. Upon his retirement from the team, he said, "I have never outstayed my welcome and I don't want to outstay my welcome with the Irish job. I don't want people to start shouting, 'Oh, you should go now!' The moment I feel that, I'll go. I don't want to fall out with the Irish. I want to be well received in Ireland. I want to be accepted in Ireland as part of Ireland."

## Sun Worshipers in a Rainy Land

AS HARD AS it may be to believe during the frequent gales and soft days of rainy weather in Ireland, the ancient Celts may actually have been sun worshipers. It wasn't that the climate was any different. It was just that, as farmers and herdsmen, they depended upon knowledge of the seasons, and that meant paying attention to the passing of the sun through the heavens. Baltinne, on the first of May, was a celebration of the coming of summer and the beginning of the growing season.

Stone circles, which probably helped the ancients keep track of the sun's voyage, can still be found scattered throughout Ireland.

GOD'S HELP is nearer than the door.

—*IRISH PROVERB*

## Of Politics and Fruit

IN CORK, the best-known supporter of longtime Irish politician Eamon De Valera was fruit vendor Molly Owens. She was a massive woman who used to have an apple stand in downtown Cork and would always have De Valera posters and banners hanging outside her house. Kids teased her by yelling out, "Up Cosgrove!" referring to De Valera's arch vote-getting opponent. Owens would take her apples and throw them at the offenders. Of course, the youngsters then scampered off, delighted with their catch of fresh apples.

## A Sore Point

ST. PATRICK MAY not actually have driven the snakes from Ireland, but he certainly carried with him a formidable weapon. The great saint carried a bishop's staff, a tall, heavy shaft called the Bachall Isu, or the Staff of Jesus.

He carried it with him as he made his way across Ireland preaching, sermonizing, and converting the Irish to Christianity. At its lower end, the staff featured a sharp metal tip, so that Patrick could easily drive it into the ground and leave the staff standing unaided.

In Munster, St. Patrick was met by King Aengus, who was eager to be baptized by the great saint. Patrick obliged, though in the midst of this solemn ritual, he accidentally drove the staff down through the king's foot. Incredibly, the king uttered not a word of complaint during the ceremony. He later explained that he thought the stabbing was just a part of the baptism.

## A Hero on Two Continents

COMMODORE JAMES BARRY is credited with being the "Father of the American Navy" because of his supervision of the Colonial fleet during the Revolutionary War. He was considered a brilliant strategist, second only to John Paul Jones. After the war, he commanded the 44-gun *United States* in the war against Algerian pirates. Barry was born in Tacumshane, County Wexford, in 1745, and died in Philadelphia in 1803. In 1956, the United States government erected a statue in his honor in his hometown in Ireland.

MAY YOU LIVE as long as you want
and never want as long as you live!

—*IRISH TOAST*

WOULD THE WORLD ever have been made if its maker had been afraid of making trouble? Making life means making trouble.

—*GEORGE BERNARD SHAW,* PYGMALION

## A Real Catch

THE RIVER SUIR, which winds through the counties of Tipperary and Waterford before joining with the rivers Nor and Barrow, is considered by many to offer the finest trout waters in all of Ireland. The local inhabitants are so enamored with the generosity of their river, they have erected a 20-foot-tall statue of a leaping trout on the main road between Cashal and Cahir.

SAINT PATRICK WAS a gintleman,
he came of decent people,
In Dublin town he built a church,
and upon't put a steeple;
His father was a Callaghan,
his mother was a Brady,
His aunt was an O'Shaughnessy,
his uncle was a Grady.

—*ZOZIMUS, "SAINT PATRICK WAS A GINTLEMAN"*

DEEP PEACE OF the running waves to you.
Deep peace of the flowing air to you.
Deep peace of the smiling stars to you.
Deep peace of the quiet earth to you.

Deep peace of the watching shepherds to you.
Deep peace of the Son of Peace to you.

—*OLD GAELIC PRAYER*

MAY YOU BE blessed
with the strength of heaven—
the light of the sun and the
radiance of the moon
the splendor of fire—
the speed of lightning—
the swiftness of wind—
the depth of the sea—
the stability of earth and the firmness of rock.

—*FROM "PATRICK'S BREASTPLATE," ATTRIBUTED TO ST. PATRICK*

HEALTH AND LONG life to you.
The wife (or husband) of your choice to you.
A child every year to you.
Land without rent to you.
And may you be half-an-hour in heaven
before the devil knows you're dead.

—*IRISH TOAST*

A TROUT IN the pot
is better than a salmon in the sea.

—*IRISH PROVERB*

WE HAVE NO time in Ireland for a man who doesn't waste both his money and his time.

—*STANDFORD AND MACDOWELL,* MAHAFFY

MAY YOU BE poor in misfortune,
rich in blessings,
slow to make enemies,
quick to make friends.
But rich or poor, quick or slow,
may you know nothing but happiness
from this day forward.

—*IRISH TOAST FOR THE BACHELOR*

I ARISE today
Through the strength of the love of Cherubim,
In obedience of angels,
In the service of archangels,
In hope of resurrection to meet with reward,
In prayers of patriarchs,

In predictions of prophets,
In preaching of apostles,
In faiths of confessors,
In innocence of holy virgins,
In deeds of righteous men.

—*FROM "PATRICK'S BREASTPLATE," ATTRIBUTED TO ST. PATRICK*

LEAVE THE flurry
To the masses;
Take your time
And shine your glasses.

—*OLD IRISH VERSE*

I'D RATHER BE an Irishman than an Englishman; but then, who wouldn't?

—*GEORGE BERNARD SHAW*

CHARACTER IS better than wealth.

—*IRISH PROVERB*

# Glorious Words and Music

A TUNE IS more lasting than the song of the birds, and a word is more lasting than the wealth of the world.

—*IRISH PROVERB*

## Vaudeville Irish

IN EARLY VAUDEVILLE, acts predominantly featured "stage" Irish fighting and drinking. But sentimental songs sprouted as a new form of entertainment in the early twentieth century. Such tunes as "Mother Machre" were written by Rida Johnson Young in 1910. The words, *Mathair mo croi,* "my loved mother" in Gaelic, certainly attracted many a listener.

The Irishness of the music was all on the surface in this new wave of entertainment. Jewish immigrant musicians had taken hold of the fad for Irish songs and very quickly learned what made a good tune. One of the most famous "Irish" tunes, "Finnegan's Wake," was actually produced in San Francisco. Other well-known songs not original to the Irish are "Danny Boy," by Fred Weatherly in 1913, "It's a Long, Long Way to Tipperary," by Jack Judge and Harry H. Williams in 1912, and "Ireland Must be Heaven, Because My Mother Came From There," written by Joe McCarthy, Fred Fischer, and Howard Johnson in 1916.

THIRST IS THE end of drinking and sorrow the end of drunkenness.

—*IRISH PROVERB*

IT'S EASIER TO improve talent in an enthusiastic musician than to create enthusiasm in a talented musician.

—*MUSICIAN PHIL COULTER*

YOU NEVER BET enough on a winning dog.

—*BOOKMAKER AT QUEEN'S PARK, BELFAST*

IT'S A LITTLE like a first date.

—*MUSICIAN PHIL COULTER, REFLECTING ON WHAT HE THINKS WHEN WALKING OUT ON STAGE FOR EACH OF HIS PERFORMANCES*

WE POETS SHOULD die of loneliness but for women, and we choose our men friends that we may have somebody to talk about women with.

—*WILLIAM BUTLER YEATS, IN* IRISH LITERARY PORTRAITS *BY W.R. RODGERS*

## Thoughts from Galway

FLAUTIST JAMES GALWAY is considered Belfast's golden boy because of his classical performances and recordings. He is always ready and eager to conquer new musical worlds. Galway began performing in a street band during his growing-up years along Carnelea Street in West Belfast. There was always music in his home, with his dad—a shipyard worker—and his mom encouraging him to practice. From those humble beginnings, he moved on to the Royal College of Music in London, London's Guildhall School, the Paris Conservatoire, and then more private studies.

Galway later performed with the Royal Shakespeare Theatre, Sadler's Wells Opera Company, the London Symphony, the BBC Symphony Orchestra, the Royal Philharmonic, and the Berlin Philharmonic. In 1975, Galway soloed. He has since appeared on major international stages and produced dozens of recordings. Some years, he does more than 120 concerts.

The sectarian religious issues of his home country often come up for Galway. But he has come to terms with his own spirituality, looking at it from a different side.

"I'm not really the churchgoing type. I'm more 'non-denominational,'" he quickly smiles when asked. "Yet I'm religious, at least deep inside. Every Irish kid is brought up in a religious way," Galway explains, saying that he reads the Bible daily.

In this vein, one of the flautist's favorite pieces is the popular "Danny Boy," a tune he says is "music touched by God, a musical Lord's Prayer."

"Even some people who don't know the words are hushed and some are brought to tears. There is just something in that simple tune that does that," he continues.

In 1977, Galway was seriously injured on a tour and almost died after an accident in which both his legs were broken. "It makes you think, gives you pause. Gloriously, my life was spared. So now when I play, it's kind of like my secret sign language with God."

LOVE LOVES to love love.

—*JAMES JOYCE,* ULYSSES

TIME IS A good storyteller.

—*IRISH PROVERB*

IT IS IN the cultivation of music that I consider the proficiency of the Irish people to be worthy of commendation. And in this their skill is, beyond all comparison, beyond that of any nation I have ever seen. For theirs is not the slow and heavy style of melody, but rapid and abrupt, yet, at the same time, sweet and pleasing in its effect.

—*GERALDUS CAMBRENSIS,*
*A MONK FROM BRITAIN (1186)*

THE WEARER BEST knows where the shoe pinches.

—*IRISH PROVERB*

THE PEN'S TRACE remains
though the hand that held it dies.

—*IRISH PROVERB*

THE PLAY WAS a great success,
but the audience was a total failure.

—*OSCAR WILDE, COMMENTING ON THE FIRST PERFORMANCE OF HIS PLAY,*
LADY WINDEMERE'S FAN

BUT I, BEING poor, have only my dreams;
I have spread my dreams under your feet;
Tread softly because you tread on my dreams.

—*WILLIAM BUTLER YEATS,*
HE WISHES FOR THE CLOTHS OF HEAVEN

ART IS THE most intense mode of
individualism that the world has known.

—*OSCAR WILDE,*
SOUL OF MAN UNDER SOCIALISM

## A Cradle of Talent

PERHAPS NO OTHER place on earth has produced so many talented musicians as the northern coast of Donegal. The Gaeltacht region, where the Irish language is still spoken, has given Irish music fans the likes of the singer Enya and the groups Clannad and Altan.

"I am asked all the time what is it about Donegal that generates this," said Mairead Ni Mhaonaigh (pronounced "nee WEE nee"), Altan's cofounder, speaking with music reviewer John Mooney of *The Irish American Post*. "I would have to say it's a mixture of the people and the rugged terrain. When I was growing up, people there had a hard time economically," Ni Mhaonaigh explained.

"Anyone wanting to go somewhere had to work for it. That's very much in the grain of Donegal, whether the field is music or the academic world," she said. Ni Mhaonaigh knows about both professions, since she and her late husband, Frankie

Kennedy, were school teachers when they formed Altan. The name is drawn from that of an Irish lake. Altan has been a leader in presenting some of the most exciting traditional Irish music coming out of Ireland from the mid-1980s through the 1990s.

## The Critic

THE POET PROCLAIMED himself of epic proportions,
Undaunted,
As he perched on the stool and read
Flannery, he in the back row, slowly rose
Like the King of Leinster, he was, shaking his fist
And demanding restitution for having to sit
through it all

—*MARTIN RUSSELL*

THE LANGUAGE OF Erin is brilliant as gold;
It shines with a lustre unrivalled of old.
Even glanced at by strangers by whom 'tis unknown
It dazzles their eyes with a light all its own!

—*JAMES CLARENCE MANGAN,*
*"THE IRISH LANGUAGE"*

## Song for the Celts

THE ANCIENT CELTS were a warlike people who swarmed out of a vast unknown portion of Asia to move in a human wave across Europe, eventually sweeping across the Irish Sea to their final outpost of Ireland. The Celts were an aristocratic race, with a great degree of political unity under a single king, as well as a federation of minor lords. They supposedly fought alongside the Greeks, battled the Romans, conquered the Germans, and flowed across Spain in a rush of music and swords.

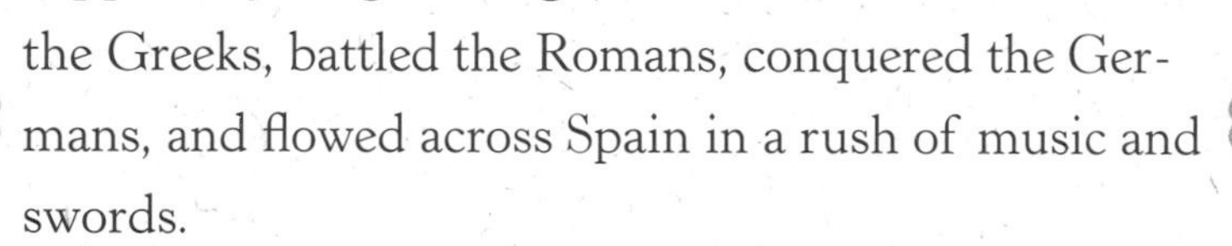

The poet D'Arcy McGee sang of them in a long hymn of praise entitled "The Celts" that starts like this:

Long, long ago beyond the misty space
Of twice a thousand years,
In Erin old there dwelt a mighty race,
Taller than Roman spears;
Like oaks and towers they had a giant grace,
Were fleet as deers

With winds and waves they made their 'biding place,
These western shepherd seers.

TO HAVE SEEN Ireland forms an event in one's life, so beautiful is it, and so unlike all other beauties that I know of. Were such beauties lying upon English shore, it would be a world's wonder: perhaps if it were on the Mediterranean, or the Baltic, English travelers would flock to it by hundreds; why not come and see it in Ireland.

—*WILLIAM MAKEPEACE THACKERAY*

## Where My Books Go

ALL THE WORDS that I gather,
And all the words that I write,
Must spread out their wings untiring,
And never rest in their flight,
Till they come where your sad, sad heart is,
And sing to you in the night,
Beyond where the waters are moving,
Storm darkened or starry bright.

—*WILLIAM BUTLER YEATS*

## Bringing the Sheep Home

SHEEP FLOWING like ghost salmon
Down the Ballybunion Road
Eddies, swirls, pools of wool
Down from the high pasture
Tooth-cropped close to the rocks
Black and white dogs snapping at tiny heels
Making the sheep dance a hornpipe along the gravel
Sprayed with the shepherd's vibrant mark
Red, blue, green
Wool matted until the shearer does his swift work
Now it's toward the sheds where the men wait
Clippers in hand, strong arms
Loud with joking, pushing, sweat-stained caps low
The farmgirls flock close to the doors and windows
Peering through the sunflecked dust
Red hair flying, swirling, twirling
Watching the men taking bets
And placing their own
Laughing

—*MARTIN RUSSELL*

## Irish Speakers

ACCORDING TO THE 1991 census in the Republic of Ireland, some 1,095,830 persons can speak Irish. In

Northern Ireland, 79,000 say they can read, write, and speak Irish. Another 63,000 indicate they have some working knowledge of the language.

THE GROVES of Blarney
They look so charming,
Down by the purling
Of sweet, silent brooks.

—*RICHARD ALFRED MILLIKEN, "THE GROVES OF BLARNEY"*

NOW COYLY RETIRING, now boldly advancing,—
Search the world all around,
from the sky to the ground,
No such sight can be found as an Irish lass dancing!

—*JOHN FRANCIS WALLER, "DANCE LIGHT, FOR MY HEART IT LIES UNDER YOUR FEET"*

WON'T YOU COME into the garden?
I would like my roses to see you.

—*SPOKEN TO A YOUNG LADY, ATTRIBUTED TO RICHARD BRINSLEY SHERIDAN*

MY MOTHER USED to tell me how I would sit around tapping my feet to the Irish music while my sisters practiced their dancing. When I was three, I went to my first dance class and I haven't stopped dancing since.

—*COLIN DUNNE, STAR OF* RIVERDANCE

ANYONE WHO HAS lived in real intimacy with the Irish peasantry will know that the wildest sayings and ideas in this play are tame indeed, compared with the fancies one may hear in any little hillside cabin in Geesala, or Carraroe, or Dingle Bay.

—*JOHN MILLINGTON SYNGE, INTRODUCTION,* THE PLAYBOY OF THE WESTERN WORLD

WE IRISH ARE too poetical to be poets; we are a nation of brilliant failures, but we are the greatest talkers since the Greeks.

—*OSCAR WILDE*

THESE THINGS I warmly wish for you—
Someone to love,
Some work to do,
A bit o' sun
A bit o' cheer
And a guardian angel
Always near.

—*OLD IRISH GREETING*

THERE'S MUSIC IN the Irish names—
Kilkenny... Tipperary...
There's beauty in the countryside,
From Cork to Londonderry,
And whoever makes his earthy home
Close to the Irish sod
Has found a bit of Heaven
And walks hand in hand with God.

—*IRISH BLESSING*

THERE IS NO language like the Irish
for soothing and quieting.

—*JOHN MILLINGTON SYNGE*

## Celtic Connections

MUSICIAN CARLOS NUÑEZ comes from the Galician region of Spain, a hilly, verdant spot on the northwest coast of the country Nuñez refers to as "Ireland with the sun."

Nuñez himself plays the gaita, a Galician bagpipe best described as a cross between Irish and Scottish pipes. He may be among the best Galician pipists in the world, which is how he came to be touring with the Chieftains, Ireland's premier traditional folk band.

It was on a concert swing through the Americas that Nuñez and the Chieftains discovered just how pervasive and widespread Celtic music is. Latin America is peopled with Spaniards, many of them exiles from Spain during the years of Francisco Franco's reign, when the dictator attempted to instill a single national identity by stamping out other cultures, including the ancient Celtic culture in Galicia.

In Havana, Nuñez met a man who may be the world's oldest bagpipe player. It didn't take much prodding from Nuñez and Chieftains lead Paddy

Moloney to convince the 100-year-old ex-Spaniard to break out his gaita and play a few songs for the visitors. He performed several old tunes, melodies from long ago, ones he had heard back in Galicia when he was but a youth. Nuñez was delighted by this rare glimpse at his own musical heritage, but Moloney was simply astonished.

"After each melody," Nuñez reports, "Paddy would say, 'I know that tune, that's an Irish tune!' "

It seems the Chieftains, who have been justly heralded as Ireland's musical ambassadors to the world, had some ancient forerunners.

NO CAUSE is utterly lost so long as it can inspire heroic devotion. No country is hopelessly vanquished whose sons love her better than their lives.

—*ABBE MAC-GEOGHEGAN, CHAPLAIN OF THE IRISH BRIGADE, WHICH FOUGHT WITH THE KINGS OF FRANCE IN THE EARLY 1700S*

THE DAWN ON the hills of Ireland!
God's angels lifting the night's black veil
from the fair, sweet face of my sireland!

—*JOHN LOCKE*

# Irish Chuckles and Groaners

Should one be anything
but deadly serious about
a matter so delicate as
the "Irish sense of humour"?

—*Cyril Cusack*,
The Humor is on Me

## A Little Wildlife Humor

A PANDA LUMBERS into The Quays pub in the Temple Bar district of Dublin, just off the Liffey River and behind the Ireland International News Agency. The bulky animal sits down, orders a deliciously foaming pint of stout and a full meal. It sits back in its chair, listening to Mickey Finnegan in the upstairs lounge playing the "Bearhaven Lassies" on his concertina. After this wonderfully leisurely supper and delightful musical interlude, the panda gets slowly up out of its chair.

From its pocket, the animal pulls out a water pistol and begins squirting it all over the place as the patrons look on in amazement. The stream breaks glasses, hits a mirror, shatters some plates, and cracks the front window. The panda then strolls out the front door, after flipping a few pound notes on the table to pay for its dinner.

Diarmaid, the pub keeper, roars out, "Hey, panda. What's the big idea!" Himself, of course, is quite incensed at having to clean up the mess.

Your man, the panda, turns and looks at Diarmaid and coolly says, "Look it up."

Being the literary sort, as are all Dublin publicans, Diarmaid pulls out his dictionary—which he just happens to have tucked behind the ornate bar. Putting on his glasses, he reads, "A panda is a small, white and black bear-like animal, native to the Himalayas. A giant panda can be up to six feet long."

But the dictionary's kicker line was, "It eats shoots and leaves."

FROM THE DAY you marry, your heart will be in your mouth and your hand in your pocket.

—*IRISH PROVERB*

ONE MAY LIVE without one's friends, but not without one's pipe.

—*IRISH PROVERB*

## Good Business Advice

O'HARA THE butcher was telling some trade secrets to his new apprentice. "If somebody comes in and wants to know the price of a leg o'mutton, you say 'five pounds.' Watch them very carefully. If they don't wince, at least like Mrs. Mulligan always does, you can then say, 'and seventy-five pence.' If they still don't twitch, you can say, 'each one!'"

BOTH YOUR FRIEND and
your enemy think you will die.

—*IRISH PROVERB*

EVERY TERRIER IS bold in his own doorway.

—*IRISH PROVERB*

NOBODY KNOWS WHERE his sod of death is.

—*IRISH PROVERB*

## City Experiences

IN A BACK table at Bewely's Oriental Café on Dublin's Grafton Street, Molly is talking with her friend Bridget. Both are legal secretaries taking a well-earned break in the late afternoon. Lamenting the hazards that shapely young ladies encounter during the rush hour along O'Connell Street, Molly says, "Riding the bus is like a religious experience. It always starts with a laying on of the hands!"

LONG AS THE day is, night comes.

—*IRISH PROVERB*

## Can't Live With 'Em, Can't Live Without 'Em

THE TWO SLIGO shopgirls are discussing their former boyfriends. The first says, "Stuck-up! Thinks about himself all the time! I couldn't get in a word edgewise, he was so full of himself."

The second girl tosses in, "You think that's conceited! My Mickie put on ten pounds just by swallowing his pride!"

## Grave Humor

THERE ARE MANY comic lines delivered at Jurey's Cabaret, the well-known nightclub in Jurey's Hotel on Pembroke Road, Ballsbridge. The following is always guaranteed for a horse laugh.

**Q:** What makes the hearse horse hoarse?

(suitable pause)

**A:** The coffin.

## Office Politics

OVERHEARD IN THE White House pub and restaurant in Kinsale, as one businessman was talking to another, "Whenever I want to kill time, I call a committee meeting. It's the ideal weapon."

THAT'S AS WELL said, as if I had said it myself.

—*JONATHAN SWIFT,* POLITE CONVERSATION

DO ENGINE DRIVERS, I wonder,
eternally wish they were small boys?

—*BRIAN O'NOLAN,* THE BEST OF MYLES

## Corny, but Cute

**Q.** WHAT IS green and stays out all night on the lawn?

**A.** Paddy O'Furniture

OUR IRISH blunders
are never blunders of the heart.
—*MARIA EDGEWORTH,* ESSAY ON THE IRISH BULLS

*Is binn béal 'na thost.*
A silent mouth is melodious.
—*IRISH PROVERB*

## Line Up!

THE YOUNG IRISH Bostonian, who came from a grand family of eight strapping boys and three girls, recalled his childhood days. "When we went to summer camp, everyone knew we came from a big family. From force of habit, we'd even stand in line outside empty bathrooms!"

## A Welcome Closer

"I SEE THAT me time is up and I appreciate your applause," said the fellow running for council in West Clare. "So I will end me talk on an appreciative note. I'll close me mouth."

## Air Woes

THE JOKE AROUND Dublin airport is that the air traffic is so heavy, the flight controllers are using a new technique to warn planes. Every time a jet departs, they yell, "Fore!"

## Hot Air

DINTY MULLIGAN THE butcher is complaining about undertaker Rory Finnegan's expansive, well-publicized ego. "Conceited!" Mulligan snorts. "You bet. Finnegan's got the only head in Munster with stretch marks!"

## Holiday Wisdom

GRANDPA DOOLAN always had this word of advice for his children and, ultimately, his 17 grandkids and four great-grandkids. "At Christmas, never stand under a partridge in a pear tree. You may get more than the Christmas spirit on you!"

THIS STONE WAS raised by Sarah's lord,
Not Sarah's virtues to record—
For they're well known to all the town,
But it was raised to keep her down.

—*AN IRISH EPITAPH IN KILMURRY, COUNTY CLARE*

YOU'LL SEE O'Ryan any night
Amid the constellations.

—*CHARLES GRAHAM HALPINE, "IRISH ASTRONOMY"*

## Never Try Baiting an Irishman

THREE ENGLISHMEN ON holiday are drinking in a pub in the bustling Temple Bar nightclub district of Dublin. They're having a grand time away for the weekend, pounding each other on the back when one tells a joke, roaring and laughing, and generally causing quite a stir in the pub.

An Irishman quietly comes in and selects a table near the three Englishmen. He pulls out a chair and eases himself into it. With a nod and slight wave to the pub keeper, the Irishman orders a pint. When it is delivered, he takes a long, slow sip. Satisfied, he sits back in his chair with a contented sigh. Reaching out, he takes another drink.

One Englishman—a big, burly fellow from Lancaster—nudges the others with his massive elbow. He peers over at the Irishman and says, "Watch this. I'll show you how to get his goat."

The first Englishman walks up to the Irish fellow and teases, "I hear your St. Patrick is a sissy."

No response. The Irishman just continues with his drink, happily taking another sip as if he never heard the wisecrack. He stares straight ahead, over to where some other patrons are playing a round of darts.

"Ah, you just don't know how to do it," scoffs the second Englishman, a skinny little Londoner. "Watch this, mates," he chuckles. Adjusting his coat and tie, the second Englishman strolls over to the Irishman and says, "I heard your St. Patrick is a goofball."

No response. Once again, the Irishman coolly takes another sip from his frothy pint. He licks his lips in satisfaction.

Frustrated, the second Englishman returns to his chair and mutters, "I guess he must be deaf."

But the third man, a medium-size gent from Essex, gets up and says, "Ah, he's just ignoring you. Listen to what I'm gonna tell him. This will really get him angry."

So the man goes over to the Irishman and says, "I heard that your St. Patrick is an Englishman."

And the Irishman finally turns away from his pint and looks up at the last Englishman and says, "Ah, so that's what your mates were trying to tell me."

**T**WO SHORTEN the road.

—*IRISH PROVERB*

## Irish Riddles

THE IRISH ARE great ones for a riddle. Here are a few—see if you can figure them out!

I ran and I got,
I sat and I searched,
If I could get it, I would not bring it with me,
And as I got it not I brought it.
(A thorn in the foot)

You see it come in on the shoulders of men,
Like a thread of silk, it will leave us again.
(Smoke)

In the garden's a castle with hundreds within,
Yet, though stripped to my shirt, I would never fit in.
(An anthill)

I threw it up as white as snow,
Like gold on a flag it fell below.
(An egg)

A blade's edge, wind, and love.
(Three things that will never be seen)

OLD MEN AND comets have been reverenced for the same reason; their long beards, and pretences to fortell events.

—*JONATHAN SWIFT*

THE ONLY CURE for love is marriage.

—*IRISH PROVERB*

O'SHAUGHNESSY THE SHOPKEEPER purchased a tub of freshly made butter from Mrs. Quinn, who owned three cows. He weighed it carefully, and then turned to the woman, his face grim.

"Mrs. Quinn, you told me the butter weighs nine pounds. My scales show it to weigh only seven. 'Tis sorry I am to say this, but you cheated me."

"Chated ye, did I, ye spalpeen?" cried Mrs. Quinn in a furious voice. "I'll have ye know I weighed that butther aginst the nine pounds iv soap ye sowld me last week!"

—*ANONYMOUS, CIRCA 1840*

WHO LIES DOWN with dogs will get up with fleas.

—*IRISH PROVERB*

HERE'S A health
To your enemies' enemies!

—*IRISH TOAST*

IN A COUPLE of hours' talk, an Englishman will give you his notions on trade, politics, the crops, the hounds or the weather. It requires a long sitting and a bottle of wine at the least to induce him to laugh.

In two hours over a pipe, a German will be quite ready to let loose the easy floodgates of his sentiment, and confide to you the many secrets of his soft heart. In two hours a Frenchmen will say a hundred and twenty smart, witty, brilliant, false things, and will care for you not one single straw.

And in two hours, an Irishman will have allowed his jovial humor to unbutton, and gambolled and frolicked to his heart's content.

Which of these, putting Monsieur out of the question, will stand by his friend with the most constancy and maintain his steady wish to serve him? That is a question which the Englishman is disposed to decide in his own favor. But it is clear that for a stranger, the Irish ways are the pleasantest, for here he is at once made happy and at home.

—*WILLIAM MAKEPEACE THACKERAY*

TO BEGIN WITH IRELAND, the most western part of the continent, the natives are peculiarly remarkable for the gaiety and levity of their dispositions; the English, transplanted there, in time lose their serious melancholy air, and become gay and thoughtless, more fond of pleasure and less addicted to reasoning.

—*OLIVER GOLDSMITH,* A COMPARATIVE VIEW OF RACES AND NATIONS

ANYBODY CAN SYMPATHISE with the sufferings of a friend, but it requires a very fine nature to sympathise with a friend's success.

—*OSCAR WILDE,* THE SOUL OF MAN UNDER SOCIALISM

KEN: Some people don't like the Irish—I do.
BRENDAN: We're very popular amoung ourselves.

—*BRENDAN BEHAN,* BORSTAL BOY

WHEN YOUR HAND is in the dog's mouth, draw it out gently.

—*IRISH PROVERB*

THE GENERAL RULE about driving in Ireland is that if you can do something that the Gardai (police) won't see you doing, or if you don't crash into anything, it's all right.

—*IRISH MOTORIST GIVING A TIP TO AN AMERICAN VISITOR*

THREE-QUARTERS OF what the opposition says about us is lies and the other half is without any foundation in truth.

—*SIR BOYLE ROACHE IN A SPEECH TO THE IRISH PARLIAMENT*

MAY YOU HAVE nicer legs than your own under the table before the new spuds are up.

—*IRISH TOAST FOR THE BACHELOR*

HERE'S TO YOU, as good as you are.
Here's to me as bad as I am.
As good as you are and as bad as I am,
I'm as good as you are, as bad as I am.

—*IRISH TOAST*

AT A BISTRO, a chap named O'Reilly
Said: "I've heard these martinis praised heilly
But they're better by far
At the neighboring bar
Where they are mixed more smoothly and dreilly."

—*LIMERICK, ANONYMOUS*

MISFORTUNES ONE CAN endure—they come from outside, they are accidents. But to suffer for one's own faults—Ah! there is the sting of life.

—*OSCAR WILDE*

THE YOUNG ARE always ready to give those who are older than themselves the full benefit of their inexperience.

—*OSCAR WILDE*

YOU ARE now leaving the County Mayo.
Last one out please turn off the lights.
(And the first one in tomorrow please light the fire!)

—*SIGN ON THE BORDER OF MAYO*

AND IF EVER ye ride in Ireland,
The jest may yet be said:
There is the land of broken hearts,
And the land of broken heads.
—*G. K. Chesterton,* Notes to a Tourist

A MAN CANNOT be too careful
in the choice of his enemies.
—*Oscar Wilde,* The Picture of Dorian Gray

## Price Wise

THE ELDERLY WOMAN was shopping at the new supermarket in Clonmel, in County Tipperary. She brought her groceries to the checkout counter and observed the young clerk ringing up the total. When the girl handed Herself the tally, she studied it for a few minutes.

"Ah, is it all right, Ma'am?" the clerk asked.

"Miss," came the response. "It's all correct. Right? No."

IT IS THE quiet pigs that eat the meal.
—*Irish Proverb*